BLOODY BERWICK

A TALE OF YESTERDAY

Keith Ryan

Published by

**MELROSE
BOOKS**

An Imprint of Melrose Press Limited
St Thomas Place, Ely
Cambridgeshire
CB7 4GG, UK
www.melrosebooks.co.uk

FIRST EDITION

Copyright © Keith Ryan 2015

The Author asserts his moral right to
be identified as the author of this work

Cover designed by Melrose Books

ISBN 978-1-910792-01-8

Printed and bound in Great Britain by:
4edge Limited
7a Eldon Way, Eldon Way Industrial Estate
Hockley, Essex
SS5 4AD

To all the Ryans, those still with us and those not.

I love them all more than words can tell.

Contents

List of Illustrations

A very short introduction

I was born on 10th February 1958 at Castle Hills Maternity Home on the north bank of the River Tweed at Berwick-upon-Tweed.

The youngest of nine children to my mam and dad, Frances and James, I was brought up in Dean Drive in Prior Park, a council housing estate started during and completed after World War II. My dad was born in an Edinburgh Leith Street tenement, just a few minutes' walk from Waverley Station. He had Irish Ryan and Scottish Stewart (if you prefer, Stuart) blood coursing through his veins. My mam was born of old Berwick stock, an Ainslie on her father's side and a Purvis (interchangeably, Purves) on her mother's. In strict chronological order, these are my brother and sisters: Jeanette, Perry, James, Rhoda, Brenda, Derek, Alan and Michael. Like all families, we have experienced bereavement as an integral part of life. My parents, and James and Derek are no longer with us. I've added to the clan over the years and with my wife Hilary, who, in my less sensible moments, perhaps wishes she was still a Smith, we have two now adult children, Frances and Michael.

On leaving school at eighteen, I also left Berwick. Over the years since, I have mislaid my Berwick accent, a fact I am reminded of every time I visit the town, but never my affection for my place of birth. I say mislaid, not lost, because accent and dialect remain buried deep within me, bursting to break through to the surface at the first opportunity: oot, not out; doon, not down, aye not yes; owld not old.

That's all very well, Keith, I hear you say, but what is the book all about? Well, it is an account of the history of Berwick, starting in medieval times with the death of Alexander III of Scotland in 1286, and ending in 1624, following the union of the crowns of England and Scotland, with the completion of a stone bridge (known now as the 'Old Bridge') over the Tweed. It is a history of the town regularly changing hands between the two kingdoms, told principally by reference to the leading characters, still well known today, including, on the English side, Edwards I to IV and Richard III, and, on the Scottish side, William Wallace and Robert the Bruce. I hope when reading it you'll be able to forgive my occasional references to the more contemporary musical and sporting loves of my life, inserted as they came to me while putting pen to paper.

I also, mischievously you might think, consider Berwick's current constitutional status. Is the town really in England, or might it, after all, be in Scotland? Mind you, on the 28th day of January 1967, Berwick was in neither Scotland nor England; it was lifted up to Heaven on clouds of black and gold, and I should know because, along with thirteen thousand three hundred and sixty four other souls, including my dad, Michael and Derek, I was witness to the miracle.

A first note of thanks before we begin: to Messrs Andy Setters and Richard Downing, who acted as my unofficial editors-in-chief; and to Ken and Claire Bush, who volunteered to road test the Halidon Hill and Walls walks.

A word of appreciation also for my good friend Laszlo Blaskovics, whose skill and expertise you will see in the pencil drawings herein. If you would like to see them in all their glory all you have to do is visit my *bloodyberwick.com* website.

Right then, here we go on our journey through the past.

Keith Ryan

Chapter One
All the World's a Stage

All the world's a stage, and all the men and women merely players:
they have their exits and their entrances

The Stage

Bloody Berwick: to some, a remote frontier town in the far north-eastern corner of England; to others, Scotland's lost crown jewel. Our stage is a place and a time; a royal burgh, no less, in a period of tumult and near continual warfare in the several centuries from the death of one of Scotland's greatest kings to the construction of what we now know as the Old Bridge over the River Tweed in the early years of the seventeenth century upon the succession, marvellously ironically, to the throne of England of another Scottish king. It is a stage on which players whose names and exploits resonate still have their entrances and exits. Together, they bequeath to Berwick a history few other towns or cities can match. And all the while, as the events unfold before it, the Tweed flows, an indifferent, disinterested witness, occasionally, if our chroniclers are to be believed, washing the red blood of battle out of the estuary into the cold, unwelcoming North Sea.

History books can be difficult to read. When you're 500 pages in with 500 still to go and you come across the umpteenth Earl of Somewhereoranother you tend to forget who's who, where you started, and what's going on. Better to leave the remaining pages for another day, which in all likelihood will never come, and turn to a less demanding task.

Well, this book isn't a thousand or even anywhere near 500 pages long, something for which I'm sure you're thankful. Nonetheless, such is the multitude of players appearing on our stage, it remains all too easy to get lost amongst them, not least because so many of them share the same name. For example, we have five English Edwards, three of them coming in a row in the early years of our story. To distinguish between them it's tempting to call them Ed, Ted, Edd, Eddie, and back to Ed, but that would be disrespectful to the English. We also have two Scottish Edwards, one Caledonian to the bone and the other desperate to be English. And, in addition, Scotland considerately serves us up with three Robert Bruces. Rob, Bob and Bobby? No, that would be disrespectful to the Scots. And seven Stewarts James. It is a blessed relief only three of them appear centre stage, and the seventh belongs to a different era.

So, before we begin, let me introduce you to a few, though by no means all, of our players, beginning in chronological order and then, I confess, going off at something of a tangent, and to our story-tellers.

The Players
Alexander III
Alexander's is the first entrance, but in truth it is his exit that interests us the most. He's the one to blame, dying when he wasn't supposed to. A great Scottish king, and a typical man. On a foul early spring night, after a drink or two too many in Edinburgh, he jumped on his horse, intent on having an amorous liaison with his young, beautiful bride and queen, Yolande, waiting patiently at home at Kinghorn castle for his return, only to fall off and die of a broken neck, leaving Scotland in turmoil and prey to the first villain of our piece, Edward I of England.

The Maid of Norway
Pity the poor maid. A child of seven. Sent from her comfortable, loving Norwegian family home to a foreign land to marry a prince from

another foreign land so the two foreign lands could become one, she didn't even survive the journey.

Edward I

This being a history book, it is, naturally, written in strictly neutral, objective terms. I visited Edward recently, at his Westminster Abbey home, just to tap gently on his tomb and have a quiet word in his ear, reminding him he wasn't – despite the inscription on his tomb: 'Edwardus Primus Scottarium Malleus Hic Est 1308 Pactum Serva' – the hammer he thought he was. To be fair to him, as everyone seems to say these days, it wasn't his idea; the words were inscribed several centuries after his death. He has, nonetheless, an awful lot to answer for, and we shall from time to time refer to him as the Hammer. The meaning of the inscription? 'Here is Edward I, Hammer of the Scots. Keep faith.'

John Balliol

King John of Scotland. He gets a mention on the plaque above Berwick's railway station steps. He was the winner in the Great Cause, of which you'll read more in Chapter Three if you make it that far. The Scots don't like John. Toom Tabard they call him – you'll have to read the chapter if you want to know what it means, or cheat by Googling it. A word on the pronunciation of his surname. Coming from Berwick, my view is that it should be bal-e-ol. However, on the BBC it is invariably bale-e-ol, and bale-e-ol it is at the Oxford University College of that name. They must be right, except in Berwick.

Robert Bruce no. 1

Our first Robert. He was the loser in the Great Cause, and none too happy about it. In serious history books he is referred to as the Competitor, so we'll do the same. Though he aspired to be king of Scotland, his principal allegiance was to Edward I.

William Wallace

No introduction needed. You've seen Braveheart; if you haven't, shame on you. For us he's Wallace, or occasionally *the* Wallace for emphasis, walking like a giant across our stage.

Robert Bruce no. 2

Our second Robert Bruce. Unlike his father, the Competitor, and his son, the really famous one, historians haven't given this Robert a moniker. He is generally referred to as his father's son or his son's father, or both. Like his father, but not his son, he asked Edward in the politest of terms if he could be king of Scotland. Edward didn't reply quite as politely. And, when it comes to Berwick, this Robert has blood on his hands, too.

Edward II

This is the one beloved of all Scots, he who was sent homeward tae think again, from Bannockburn via Bamburgh and Berwick. He actually spent a considerable amount of time in Berwick, mainly because it was about as far away from London as he could get and still be in England, until 1318 at least. With one exception, a certain Piers Gaveston, whom perhaps Edward liked a little too much, he didn't have a great deal of time for his barons, and they had even less time for him.

Robert Bruce no. 3

Our third, and truly great, Robert. Now, you would think, especially in the fourteenth century, when you could be hanged for the most trivial of misdemeanours, that anyone who murdered a nobleman and simultaneously violated the sanctity of a church would not live to see many more dawns. But not this Robert. He grabbed the Scottish throne instead. Learning from the mistakes of his father and grandfather, he didn't bother to ask Edward first. He just took it. Some see him as a usurper, with good reason because that's exactly what he was. Most people, including me, know him as Robert *the* Bruce, but proper historians, in proper history books, never say Robert *the* Bruce. Too low brow for them I suspect, although a few compromise by now and again referring to him as *the* Bruce, with no mention of his first name. So what shall we do? We'll keep it simple. To us he is merely Robert.

The Two Robin Hood kings

You know who I mean, the Lionheart and his malicious, despicable no-good brother. They turn up on stage a century too early, meaning this is both their entrance and exit. First up is the good King Richard, downing a flagon, and some more, of the local ale when handing Berwick to Scotland in return for 10,000 marks to be used in funding his Holy Land crusade. Next comes the evil King John, spending the night in the town after indulging in a little cross-border marauding, and rewarding its inhabitants by burning it to the ground, starting with the B&B that had played host to him. Where was Robin when we needed him? Probably in Sherwood Forest, disguised as Einstein, cavorting with Maid Marion. In the interests of historical accuracy, I ought to say these two little snippets are absolutely true.

Harry Potter

No, I lie. Sadly, he makes neither an entrance nor an exit. It did occur to me an appearance might boost sales, and with Harry's help we, together, might have solved the biggest mystery of all; how was it that Hermione ended up in the arms of Ron Weasley? Sorry, JK, that was the one plot line it was just too implausible to believe. Again, in the interests of historical accuracy, regrettably, Harry remains in Hogwarts. Generally, in fact, wizards and witches are rather thin on the ground. There are only two of note; a Dunbar soothsayer with a message of warning for Alexander, and a misogynist apparition, said to have been in the form of a man with shoulder length yellow hair and dressed in a blue gown, whom we shall meet on the way to Flodden Field.

Edward Balliol and Edward III

Oh dear, two Edwards on stage at the same time. The first is our first Scottish Edward, son of King John Balliol, the Great Cause winner. This Edward is leader of the Disinherited, a collection of Scottish noblemen so embittered at their treatment at the hands of their fellow Scots they were willing to sell their souls to the English to gain advancement in Scotland. The second is our third English Edward, son of the pitiful second Edward and grandson of the Hammer. In whose footsteps will he follow? Be patient. Wait and see. All will be revealed in due course.

Paul Gascoigne

Universally acknowledged as the modern day footballing hammer of the Scots. 1996 and all that.

The Earls of Leicester

Overlooked in the chronicles and rarely mentioned by modern academics, seven earls of Leicester and two countesses are hidden in the pages herein, like silver foxes invisible against the winter snow, whispering incessantly "Berwick is in England, Berwick is in England". Centuries, they assert, of the town being on the south side of the border provide sufficient evidence of permanence; but time is an ocean, and it ends at the shore, and the constitutional position is not necessarily as straightforward as it might appear.

The Stewarts

Otherwise known as the Stewards and/or the Stuarts. There are a lot of them. Two Roberts (one of whom is really a John – King Not John) and seven Jameses. Happily, to assist in avoiding too much confusion, of the Jameses only numbers three, four and six have significant parts to play. For three, Berwick is his pride and joy, won in boyhood only to be lost in adulthood. The fourth left a haunting, silent, unmarked graveyard as his legacy, though not one occupied by him. The sixth, despite his time in the town being brief, bequeathed a treasure as much used today – almost every hour of every day – as it was upon its completion four centuries ago. By the way, my dad was a Stewart, occasionally a Stuart, on his mother's side. And his first name was James. And in his manner he was kingly; James the Eighth as far as I'm concerned.

The French
Allies of the Scots and enemies of the English (except when it suited their purposes to be allies of the English and detached, superior cousins of the Scots) the French come and go, on stage one minute and gone the next. More often imaginary than real, the 'auld alliance' of Scotland and France, which incidentally first came into existence in Berwick and Paris in 1295, against the 'auld enemy', England, occasionally has a role to play but only for short periods and without ever starring.

Les Sept Magnifiques
Not all of our players were for England or Scotland. Had the magnificent seven prevailed, notwithstanding they were all borderers, this book might have been written in French. Chapter Nine for details.

The ordinary people
That's you and me, the Berwickers, destined to suffer cruelty, massacre, violence, pillage, arson and sundry other outrages without regard to age, sex, religion or rank. That is not my description; it is the indictment of Edward I and his son contained in the Declaration of Arbroath of 1320, an exceptionally eloquent statement of Scottish nationhood and a document we shall encounter in Chapter Six. I suppose, not surprisingly, the Declaration, remarkable document though it is, is blinkered and blind to the equally cruel and callous acts committed time and time again by the Scots on the ordinary people of northern England – just ask the folk of Hexham and Durham.

The Walls

In tourist guides and other, serious publications, the Walls are either the Elizabethan Walls or Ramparts or Fortifications. To local people, and therefore in this book, they are just the Walls, deserving I'm sure you'll agree, of being respectfully awarded a capital W. Yes, I know they are not a player as such but there is no denying their character or personality. And, while all our other players have long since exited, the Walls remain, standing proudly, wrapping the town in a warm blanket of history and identity.

The Henrys

Everyone knows there were eight Henrys. Happily, only the hapless one, number six; the usurper, number four part two; and to a lesser extent and only indirectly, the grotesque one, number eight, have roles of any significance.

Richard III before he was Richard III

He is not only Shakespeare's devil usurper; for those of us born on the north side of the Tweed (and therefore truly Scottish, notwithstanding what others might say) he is the town's bête noir, the devil assuming the appearance of the Duke of Gloucester, who placed the town in English hands once and for all. Or did he? I have a dream, that one day soon, once the townsfolk have voted themselves independent, I'll visit him in his new Leicester Cathedral resting place, to let him know his work has been undone. Having consulted with the Electoral Commission, I can confirm this is the agreed referendum question:

Should Berwick once again be an independent country, free of England and Scotland? Yes/No

The Women

They are few and far between in our story. Apart from the Maid and the occasional queen, not many are seen on stage, save for the two unfortunates for years hanging in cages from the battlements of Roxburgh and Berwick castles. There is no Joan of Arc, no Jean of Arbroath, raising Edward III's siege of Berwick in July 1333 before Halidon Hill.

The Story-tellers

To these authors we are deeply, deeply indebted as they are the ones who took the trouble to tell the story.

There are some excellent books on the history of Berwick, and some equally excellent ones on Anglo-Scottish relations in the Middle Ages. For me, the pick of the bunch on Berwick are (take a deep breath, there are some long titles): John Scott's *Berwick-Upon-Tweed: The History of The Town and Guild*; Leonard George's *Berwick-upon-Tweed and the East March*; John Fuller's *The History of Berwick upon Tweed, including a short account of the villages of Tweedmouth and Spittal, &c.*; and George Ridpath's *The border-history of England and Scotland, deduced from the earliest times to the union of the two crowns. Comprehending a particular detail of the transactions of the two nations with one another; accounts of remarkable Antiquities; and a Variety of interesting ANECDOTES of the most considerable FAMILIES and distinguished CHARACTERS in both Kingdoms.* What a title. Whether it's a world record or not I can't say but what I can and do say is that it's a wonderful read. Add to the list Frederick Sheldon's *History of Berwick-Upon-Tweed ...To Which are Added Notices of Tweedmouth, Spittal, Etc.*, a shorter account than Ridpath's, but equally enjoyable. I know Tweedmouth intimately – I grew up there, in Dean Drive, spending my days as a goalie diving around in the Oval mud (the Oval, for those of you not from Berwick, is not a cricket stadium). Spittal I know equally well. Where, however, 'Etc.' might be I can't say; perhaps up around Castle Terrace, the posh part of the town, where Dean Drivers rarely venture.

There are too many of the more general books to mention by title. Just search the authors: Andrew Fisher; Colm McNamee; Simon Schama; Michael Prestwich; Seymour Phillips; Fiona Watson; Norman MacDougall; Michael Brown; Niall Barr; John Sadler; Marc Morris; and Alistair Moffat.

Of the books on Berwick, Scott's is a fine, undemanding read, but Ridpath's and Sheldon's are my favourites. Ridpath's is one long, extremely long, acerbic adventure. If you want to read it in a reasonable period of time you'll need to take two or three weeks' holiday from work or, if you've had your statutory 5.6 weeks' entitlement, develop a bad back. Sheldon is a time traveller, an eye witness to the epic events he describes with a passion. He stands on the bridge as the Wallace's remains are brought to the town for burial. And we stand next to him. With Sheldon, we see the townsfolk bare their arses to the Hammer, the Bruce riding into the town reclaiming Scotland's crown jewel at the expense of his eternal soul, and the deathly hail of English and Welsh arrows wiping out Scotland's finest a mile up the road at Halidon Hill. In our story we rely on Ridpath and Sheldon for the detail, with the context coming from the others.

I confess to having embellished a little here and there, and you may come across the occasional reference to a Bob Dylan or Neil Young song or lyric, the two musicians being exquisite and inspirational story-tellers themselves, inserted for no reason other than doing so has made me smile. And last, but someone who could never be least, the great William Shakespeare, whoever he might have been, also makes a contribution, as I'm sure you have already noted.

Chapter Two
The Fall of the House of Dunkeld

In mid-November 1251, Alexander, a mere ten years old, stepped on to our stage, crossing the Tweed from its north side along Berwick's long, narrow timber bridge into England. Young though he was, Alexander was not a boy; he was a king. He travelled as Alexander III of Scotland, having been crowned upon the Stone of Scone some two or so years previously.

During his reign of 36 years, Berwick was transformed into the economic heart of Scotland and the country's most prosperous town, enjoying the prestige of being a royal burgh alongside Edinburgh, Stirling and Roxburgh. Strong trading links, predominantly through the export of wool to northern Europe, were the town's life blood, and the presence of French, German and Flemish merchants gave it a cosmopolitan hue. Bread, wine and ale were in plentiful supply. In Scotland's time of peace it was Berwick's golden age.

Upon reaching Tweedmouth on the south side of the bridge, Alexander was met by his exalted English escorts, the Bishop of Durham together with the barons and Sheriff of Northumberland. It was their duty to accompany the king, to provide him with safe passage through the less than hospitable Northumbrian countryside, to the Tees, from where an equally prestigious company of clerics and English nobles in their turn travelled with Alexander to his destination, York.

His journey had a dual purpose. First, he was to be married. Second, he was to perform another ceremony of no less importance, concerning the personal relations between the kings of Scotland and England.

Waiting for him at York were his bride to be, Princess Margaret, and her father, King Henry III of England. Alexander arrived on Christmas Eve. On Christmas Day, he was knighted by Henry and, on 27th December, Margaret and he were married in York Cathedral amid all the splendour and excess that inevitably accompany a royal wedding. Had you attended the wedding feast, on the menu before you would have been the familiar and the unfamiliar. From supplies gathered in by the sheriffs of Cumberland, Lancaster, Lincoln and Northumberland, the Mayor of York, and the bailiffs of Scarborough and Newcastle, the wedding guests sated their appetites on 10,000 haddock and 1,000 cod, 60,000 herrings, 70 pigs (heads attached), 500 red hinds, 200 wild boars and sows, and, for good measure, 125 swans.

Once the feast was over, Henry turned to Alexander. The time had arrived for the Scottish king to perform his part in the second ceremony of the day; to pay homage to Henry and thereby cement their feudal relationship. Feudalism is foreign to us, a thing of the dim and distant past. Nevertheless, if we are going to have some understanding of what Alexander was being invited to do, we must have an appreciation, if only in passing, of how in the feudal era political, economic and military relations were inextricably linked to the personal.

The essence of the feudal relationship was that, in return for a grant of some kind, most often of land, a free man – the vassal – would voluntarily place himself under the protection, and at the service, of another free man – the lord or overlord – while even in so doing preserving his status as a free man. Feudalism, thus, revolved around the notion of free men in dependence. The vassal was no slave. He was not in any sense owned by his lord and, subject to performing the duties and obligations he had voluntarily entered into in return for the grant made to him, he was otherwise a free man.

In commending himself to his lord the vassal generally performed two acts. One was to take an oath of fealty – of fidelity – to his lord. In taking the oath, which invariably involved an appeal to God and often a simultaneous touching of a holy object of some sort (perhaps a relic or gospel), the vassal promised to be faithful to and serve his lord. The other was the act of homage; kneeling bare headed and weaponless, the vassal placed his hands inside the hands of his lord, in so doing placing himself at his lord's disposal.

In common with many Scottish nobles, Alexander held lands in England, in Cumberland and, through the Earldom and Honour of Huntingdon, in eleven other English counties. In respect of those lands Alexander had no difficulty in giving the homage sought of him, acknowledging he held them as the vassal of his now father-in-law. But Henry had another, more tacit, agenda. He was seeking something else, namely homage from Alexander for the kingdom of Scotland or, in other words, Alexander's acknowledgement that he held the kingdom only as a vassal of Henry, to whom he was subservient. This was a pivotal moment in the relations between the two monarchs and, by extension, the two kingdoms. What was Alexander to do? Henry and the might of the English nobility waited for Alexander to buckle and kneel. The Scottish wedding guests watched in silence; the status of their country hinged on words about to spring forth from the mouth of their young monarch, standing alone before England's king at the height of his powers.

Yes, Alexander said, he had conceded fealty and homage for his lands in England. And, yes, he had come to England in peace to be married to Margaret and honour Henry as his father-in-law. As, however, for Scotland, he could not concede or answer Henry's request without first having, in Scotland, held full deliberation and suitable counsel with his chief men. Not a bad reply for a ten-year-old. Wrong footed, nonplussed, Henry returned to the wedding celebrations, never to raise the subject again. At the end of December, Alexander and his entourage journeyed back to Scotland, returning to and crossing the rickety wooden bridge at Berwick, and from there travelling along the north bank of the Tweed to Roxburgh.

Alexander's line – the House of Dunkeld – stretched back over two centuries to 1034 (to before the Norman conquest of England). With his marriage to Margaret, he looked to the future with confidence; an heir would surely be produced and the line would continue to furnish Scotland with its monarchs for generations to come. Moreover, with such close ties between the dynastic families of Dunkeld and Plantagenet, Scotland would continue to prosper through peace with its southern neighbour. That confidence, it seemed, was made material in due course. The royal couple had three children: Margaret born in 1261; Alexander born in 1264; and David born in 1273. Even, however, for those of royal blood, life in the thirteenth century hung by a precious, precarious thread and, in the space of a few short years, the thread was cut. Death and extinction were stalking the House of Dunkeld.

Amid rumours of having been poisoned, Margaret senior died in 1275. Only 34 years old, suddenly Alexander was a widower, albeit comforted by the knowledge that, with three children, the succession was secure. But it wasn't. In 1280 David died. His sister, Margaret, followed in April 1283. In 1280 she had married Eric, king of Norway. She died on 9th April, only a few days after bearing a daughter, also Margaret. Say hello to the Maid of Norway. On 21st January 1284, on his 20th birthday, Alexander junior died, leaving the king a widower and childless.

Alexander's response to this sudden succession issue was to hold a colloquium at Scone. There, it was confirmed, a monarch's grandchild, boy or girl, had the right to succeed to the Scottish throne in the event of the monarch dying and leaving no immediate progeny. And it was further confirmed that it meant in this particular instance, should Alexander die in such circumstances, 'we shall all receive our illustrious child Margaret' as queen. So, at only ten months old, the child Margaret, daughter of King Eric and Queen Margaret of Norway, granddaughter of Alexander, became the acknowledged heir to the Scottish throne. She was, it must be said, the insurance, fall back option, because Alexander was still young enough to father children in a second marriage. The succession was an issue, not a crisis. His bride, in 1285, was the beautiful, vivacious, eighteen year old Yolande de Reux. Dunkeld, this time, surely, was secure. No, it wasn't.

Thomas of Earlston was a thirteenth century soothsayer. One night, in March 1286, he was at Dunbar castle, entertaining guests of the local earl. What, however, Thomas had to say was hardly entertaining, though, the gathered audience presumably reassured itself, nothing more than foolish prophecy:

> *'Woe worth the morrow, for it will be a day of disaster and woe, a very great and bitter day in the kingdom; before noon such a wind shall blow as has never been heard of for many years, and the blast of it shall humble lofty hearts and level the high places of the hills.'*

That same foul night, Alexander held counsel at Edinburgh castle. At night's end, against all good advice and acting recklessly in drink, Alexander set off on horseback for Queensferry, from where he intended to cross the Forth by ferry and, once across, ride to Kinghorn castle, for there the beautiful Yolande, whose birthday it was the following day, awaited. Riding through a tempest, he made it safely enough to Queensferry, where he persuaded a reluctant ferryman to take him across the river. On reaching the Forth's north side, off he set on horseback once more, for Kinghorn. He didn't make it. In the early daylight of his queen's nineteenth birthday, a bitter wind still blowing, he was found dead at Pettycur shore, his neck broken in consequence of having been thrown from his horse.

Now it was crisis time. Scotland was immediately thrown into turmoil. In an instant, the country had lost one of its most successful and revered kings, and in his place to ensure the continuation of the House of Dunkeld stood only his granddaughter, Margaret, a three year old Norwegian child who had never set foot in the kingdom it now appeared it was her destiny to govern.

Civil war threatened, avoided only through an uneasy alliance constructed at Scone a month or so after Alexander's death. Homage was sworn, reluctantly by some, to Margaret, the nation's illustrious child. She was acknowledged as queen. A council of six guardians was appointed, initially to govern the country until such time as the new queen could be brought to Scone for her enthronement. Their first step, taken to confirm and legitimise their authority, was the making of a new great seal. In a few short years, the seal would come to symbolise not power but weakness in the form of the impotence of Scotland's ruling elite in the face of Edward I of England's aggression.

For the most part, however, the Scottish nobility rallied around the cause of the Maid, if for no other reason than to have acted otherwise would have left the country exposed to external threats, not least that posed by Edward, the Hammer, whose reign had commenced in 1272. By the mid-1280s he had succeeded in subjugating Wales and was openly letting it be known he considered himself the feudal overlord of Scotland.

The threat Edward presented was dealt with, it seemed successfully at the time, by way of negotiations which led in July 1290 to the Treaty of Birgham (a village on the north side of the Tweed near Wark). Under the terms of the treaty, Margaret was to marry Edward's son, Edward Prince of Wales (who in years to come would suffer humiliation at Bannockburn) and, in return for this marriage between Dunkeld and Plantagenet, Scotland's legal, civil and ecclesiastical independence would be respected. Margaret, it was agreed, would arrive in Scotland by 1st November 1290. The prince, himself only a boy, was unenthusiastic about the match and was reconciled to it only by his father's insistence that a man needs a maid.

It is strange to think that, had the terms of the treaty been put into effect, the crowns of Scotland and England would have been unified some three centuries earlier than was actually the case. With unification, it might reasonably be said, would have followed a continuation of the peace which had been forged between the two countries during Alexander's reign. With commerce continuing uninterrupted and unaffected by war, Berwick would have remained a prosperous, peaceful town, perhaps even growing to city size, in no need of fortifications to fend off invading armies. Picture the town without its Walls. But it was not to be. Fate had one final tragedy in store for the House of Dunkeld, a tragedy which would soon lead to war between Scotland and England for centuries to come, with Berwick in the eye of the breaking storm.

Margaret would not be enthroned at Scone, nor would she marry Edward, Prince of Wales. She was destined to be the queen who never set foot in the land over which she reigned. History turned in September 1290 when, on her voyage to Scotland, she died as her ship reached the Orkneys. Her body was returned to Norway by the ship's captain, Thore Haakonsson, and Ingeborg Erlingsdatter, her governess. Her coffin was opened in the presence of her father, King Eric, and her remains were then placed next to her mother's in the King's Vault in Christ Church, Bergen. Pity the poor Maid.

Chapter Three
The Process of Norham and The Great Cause

Upon the Maid's death bringing to an end the House of Dunkeld, the resulting vacuum was filled with indecent haste by a rush of claimants to the vacant throne. There were fourteen in all: a couple of kings; an assortment of barons, earls and counts; and several without title who claimed, with varying degrees of plausibility, descent from one dead Scottish king or another. The two kings who threw their crowns into the ring were our villainous friend, Edward I, and Eric the Viking, the Maid's father. Edward's claim was legitimate, if not strong, in so far as he had a little Scots' royal blood running through his veins. He did not, however, pursue his claim with any vigour and soon, as we shall see, abandoned it in favour of a strategy of indirect, feudal rule. As for Eric, his claim was without foundation in law, principle or common sense. The Maid, he contended indisputably, was his daughter. If she through death was deprived of her entitlement then he in life should inherit it. Not even Eric himself took his claim seriously.

Before, however, the fine noblemen of Scotland could trot off to Scone for another enthronement, the thorny issues of who and how had to be decided. Who should settle the succession? And how and by what procedure was it to be settled? The guardians realised Edward could not be ignored. He was Alexander's brother-in-law; he was a claimant, if only nominally; and, most importantly of all, with his expansionist bent, he was a real danger to Scotland's peace and security. Better therefore, the guardians thought, to include him in the process than risk his wrath, and war, by excluding him. Appeasement was preferable to confrontation. Following that not unsound reasoning, the guardians issued an invitation to Edward to act as arbitrator between the various claimants, except of course himself as he couldn't be both judge and contender. A clever means, the guardians congratulated themselves, of involving the English king while simultaneously ensuring their kingdom would not be his to rule. It was a massive miscalculation.

Edward accepted the invitation with relish, and in so doing immediately summoned an English parliament to meet at Norham in May 1291. In the several weeks from 6th May to 12th June 1291 – in the Process of Norham – Edward manipulated events and manoeuvred himself into a position, to his satisfaction, of overlordship of Scotland. He had no need to pursue his own claim; he would rule through his appointee.

While Edward's parliament sat in the splendour of Norham castle, the Scottish nobility, already beginning to have second thoughts about involving him so pivotally in their country's affairs, gathered on the other side of the Tweed, at Upsettlington. Our story-tellers differ, principally along national lines, in their accounts of what happened next. The English chroniclers tell us Edward, exercising his rights of overlordship, summoned to him representatives from the Upsettlington Scots to hear what he had to pronounce – that Scotland was his vassal kingdom. For the Scottish chroniclers, however, there was no summons, no commandment, only an invitation to meet the English king without prejudice to Scotland's status as an independent nation.

Whatever the truth of the matter, on 10th May the assembled Scots, menaced by the thought of how Edward might apply the significant armed presence he had brought with him and the English fleet handily anchored at the mouth of the Tweed near Berwick, sent two bishops and two of the nobility across the river. They didn't stay long. Upon their arrival they were treated to a fearsome speech by Roger Brabazon, one of Edward's henchmen. His king, he explained, had come in peace (with an army and a fleet) to undertake the task asked of him. And then came the sting. This exercise Edward would conduct by virtue of his overlordship, an overlordship the four Scots in attendance were left in no doubt they were required to accept. In a strong echo, however, of the young Alexander's courageous response to Henry III, the four stood their ground. They could not, they said, answer on behalf of a king who was not yet enthroned. They had taken an oath in 1286 upon Alexander's death and would not break it nor, they implied, would they expect Edward to require them to do so. Their courage brought some relief; a three-week period of grace until 1st June, during which time the Upsettlington gathering retired to Berwick to devise a means by which they could maintain their stance of independence in the face of the all too obvious military threat on their doorstep. On 31st May Edward issued a second 'invitation' for the Scots to appear before him at Norham. On this occasion it was declined. A written reply was instead delivered by messengers. The reply was as before: Edward's claim to overlordship could not be answered until there was a Scottish king enthroned to answer it.

Frustrated though he undoubtedly was, Edward did not respond militarily to the rebuttal. Instead, he adopted a more subtle approach, turning his attention away from the uncooperative Scottish magnates towards those who would be king; the much more malleable claimants. If, on behalf of the community of the realm, the magnates would not concede overlordship, Edward was determined to have it acknowledged by different means. He therefore presented the claimants with a bleakly simple choice: either submit to him as their feudal master or be eliminated from the contest to be king.

How easy it was to manipulate the claimants, even our villain couldn't have anticipated. Over the week from 5th to 11th June, to a man (including Eric the Viking, by proxy), all those claiming right to the Scottish throne swore an oath of fealty to the English king at Norham. Shame on them. The first to capitulate was the Competitor, on

5th June. If you can't remember who the Competitor is go back to page 3. Most of the rest followed suit the next day. John Balliol was the last to submit, on 11th June.

History, by which I mean the Scots and the vast majority of Scottish historians, has not been kind to Balliol. But here at Norham, he was the only claimant to show a degree, admittedly modest, of resistance to Edward's pressing. While his co-claimants were falling over themselves to submit to Edward's overlordship rather than be ruled out of the contest for the throne, Balliol at least held out for a short while. Edward, Balliol asserted, was not overlord, but merely arbiter. But there was too much at stake. He had a meritorious claim he was unwilling to sacrifice. Thus, on 11th June he became the last of the claimants to submit, and for his pains he was given special attention by Edward. Whereas it had been sufficient for the others to swear their oath in the abbey at Norham, Balliol, in addition to that, was required to swear it before Edward himself in the king's chambers at Norham castle. This, you might think (and you would be correct to do so), gives us a clue to what was in Edward's mind.

In any event, the English king now had what he wanted; the next king of Scotland, whoever was chosen, and, by extension, the kingdom of Scotland, were Edward's to rule over. Completely undermined, the Scottish magnates, at the English king's insistence and having little choice but to accept his undertaking that he would hand them back once the country had a king, granted to him legal and physical possession of Scotland's castles. And, on 12th June at Upsettlington, the great seal of office, by which the guardians had sought to demonstrate their authority to rule in the Maid's name after her grandfather's death, was meekly surrendered to Edward. In time, he would use it to great symbolic effect.

Upon completion of the Process of Norham another quite distinct process, by which Edward would decide between the claimants, could begin. But where was the adjudication court to sit? Edward favoured

Westminster. The Scots, for once putting their timidity aside, would have none of it. The destiny of the Scottish crown – the Great Cause – would be decided on Scottish soil, at Berwick castle. Edward, somewhat surprisingly, conceded the point.

To assist him in his deliberations, the court created specifically for the purpose consisted of 104 auditors. Twenty four were appointed by Edward. Of the remaining 80, 40 were nominated by Balliol and 40 by the Competitor. The involvement of these two protagonists in this way reflected the fact that by common consent they had the strongest claims to the throne. Both men were related to the late King Alexander through his great uncle, David, Earl of Huntingdon. Balliol was the grandson of David's eldest daughter. Bruce the Competitor was the son of David's second daughter. So, the Competitor was nearer in blood to Alexander while Balliol was descended from the eldest descending royal line. It was a case of Roman law against feudal law. Roman law favoured the Competitor. Feudal law favoured Balliol.

In addition to the auditors, Edward was further assisted by a team of Dominican monks brought to Berwick from Paris and accommodated in a church adjacent to the castle. They were to provide the legal expertise required for the task ahead and were charged firstly with sifting through the historical and legal documents on which the various claimants relied. In truth, save for Balliol and the Competitor, the other claimants (Edward by this time having formally ruled himself out of the contest) were an odd collection of fantasists and no-hopers.

The court sat for the first time on 3rd August 1291. Edward, naturally, dominated the proceedings. While he was content, he explained, to grant the claimants the favour of choosing between them, he did so without prejudice to his rights and those of his heirs. In other words, the king of Scotland was to be appointed by the overlord of Scotland. Not that he was in any hurry to make the appointment. Having opened the proceedings he, within the day, adjourned them for the ostensible reason of allowing one of the claimants sufficient time to produce documentary evidence in support of his claim.

The claimant in question was one of the fantasists, Count Florence of Holland. An ancestor of his, he asserted, had been promised by King William the Lion of Scotland (Alexander's grandfather) that if ever the House of Dunkeld should fail (which it did on the poor Maid's death) the throne would pass to whomsoever at the time of such failure was the Count of Holland. Hopeless though the claim was, it just so happened that Count Florence's son had recently married Edward's daughter. And as Edward had a grip on Scotland through control of its castles, why rush the Great Cause? No, the Count would be given time; the proceedings were adjourned until Edward's next parliament, at Berwick castle, on 2nd June 1292.

It came as no surprise to any of the other claimants when, in June 1292, Count Florence was unable to produce a single document which in any way supported his claim. What was a surprise, however, was that, on recommencement of the proceedings, having been represented only by proxy at Norham, the town was graced by the presence of another royal personage. It was the Maid's father, King Eric the Viking who came calling. So anxious was he to grab the crown denied to his daughter by death that, immediately upon his arrival, he knelt before Edward and acknowledged the English king's sovereignty over the kingdom of Scotland. His claim, as we have seen, was entirely without merit of any sort but that didn't prevent him from hoping that grovelling might do the trick. While Edward was hardly likely to be persuaded by Eric's sycophancy, it remained the case that the English king was in no hurry to reach a decision, or even to separate the wheat from the chaff. Thus, Count Florence and good old Eric remained, theoretically, in the hunt when, still in June, Edward ordered a second adjournment, to 14th October.

Finally, at the third time of asking, on the second recommencement of the Cause in October, the auditors got down to the serious business of assessing the relative merits of the various claims. They first considered the claims of Balliol and the Competitor. On 6th November they delivered to Edward their unanimous opinion. Balliol, they advised, being descended from the eldest descending line, had a better claim to the throne of Scotland than the Competitor. Over the course of the next few days they dismissed, to no one's surprise, the remaining claims as having been brought with varying degrees of frivolousness. And so it was, as the plaque at Berwick railway station commemorates, that on 17th November 1292 in the Great Hall of Berwick castle, before an assembly of England's and Scotland's great and good, Edward passed judgment in the Great Cause in favour of Balliol, King John of Scotland. Just in case, however, there was any doubt as to where the real power resided, Edward, after pronouncing judgment, produced the great seal of Scotland – made for the guardians in 1291 and handed over to Edward at the conclusion of the Process of Norham – and duly broke it into four pieces, placing them in a leather bag for transportation to Westminster.

Balliol bends the knee

*Balliol bends the knee in homage to the Hammer in return for being granted the
Scottish crown. 'I'm so excited, I just can't hide it,' he says,
while the Pointer Sisters look on in admiration.*

Chapter Four
Alas, Foul Crime

The judgment in his favour in the Great Cause was one which before very long King John would reflect upon with a bitter heart, for his reign was to be marked by humiliation at every turn; in the first instance at Edward's hands, followed by abandonment and ridicule from those he now ruled over.

Edward did not wait before re-asserting feudal superiority over his vassal king of Scotland. In addition to the oath of fealty John had sworn on 17th November in the castle's Great Hall, he was required by Edward to do the same again the very next day at Norham castle, and while he was inaugurated as king on the Stone of Destiny at Scone on that most important of days for Scots – 30th November, St Andrew's Day – less than a month later, on Boxing Day 1292, he was at Newcastle paying homage to Edward yet again. Such was John's weakness, or perhaps more kindly such was the weakness of his position, that during his Christmas stay in Newcastle he found himself giving his written acknowledgement of Edward's release from any obligations the English king may still have had under the terms of the Treaty of Birgham, and from his promise made at Norham to respect Scotland's independence.

And, just as the Scottish crown was subjugated to the English crown, so, following a decree made by Edward in November 1292 while still in Berwick, was the Scottish legal system made subordinate to its English counterpart. To prove the point, in December of that year Edward and his court sat at Newcastle to hear several appeals against decisions made in the Scottish courts. Edward made it plain to the gathered Scots that, when circumstances warranted it, he considered himself entitled to require John to appear before him, in England, to explain and answer for decisions made in Scotland.

One such instance was the case of Macduff, who appealed to Edward against a judgment made by John dispossessing him of certain of his lands in Scotland. The appeal was heard at a parliament held by Edward at Westminster which the Scottish king was summoned to attend, and attend he duly did. In another, on this occasion quickly futile, echo of how the young Alexander had at his wedding feast stood up to Henry III, John sought to sidestep Edward's pressing by asserting that he, as king of Scotland, could not participate in proceedings in an English court without first consulting and obtaining advice from counsel in Scotland. But whereas Alexander's reply had disconcerted Henry, Balliol's answer had the effect only of incurring Edward's wrath. The reply was, in Edward's eyes, no reply at all and as such no defence to the appeal. Accordingly, Macduff was entitled to and received appeal judgment in his favour; the lands he had been deprived of were restored to him. As for John, Edward decreed that until such time as he purged his disobedience and contempt of the English court, three Scottish castles would be taken under Edward's direct control. The decree was not carried out; there was no need for it to be as, while still at Westminster, John submitted.

The resentment of the Scottish magnates towards Edward, combined with their frustration at John's continuing displays of weakness, festered in the several years after 1292. Ironically, what brought the countries into open conflict was Edward's feudal obligation to another king, Philip the Fair of France, to whom the English king was required to pay homage for lands he held in Gascony. In feudal law, for the lands he held in what is now France, Edward was Philip's vassal, as John was to Edward. Relations between the two kings were strained to breaking point when, in 1294, several Gascony towns and their castles fell into

Philip's avaricious hands. Edward, never one to flinch from conflict, resolved to recover them by military means through an alliance of European states whose armies would join with his in what is now northern France, from where they would move gradually south into Gascony.

It was at this point that, in the eyes of Scotland's nobility, Edward overstepped the mark. The Scottish king, Edward, demanded would meet his vassalage obligation to support the English military operation by sending men, including those of high rank, to join and fight in the Gascony campaign. Poor, hapless John found himself on the horns of a dilemma. On the one hand, to resist would in all likelihood lead him to forfeit the lands he held in England. On the other hand, acquiescence would amount to a final acknowledgement, if one were needed, of his and his kingdom's subservience to Edward. In the event, John's prevarication, for his initial response was to not respond at all, resulted in the decision being taken out of his hands. The hiatus caused by his hesitation was filled by the formation of a council of twelve of the great and good of Scotland, comprising an equal number of bishops, peers and barons, to direct John in all public affairs and to free both John and his people from the bond of fealty he had sworn to Edward. Not quite a *coup d'etat* but not far short.

Now, at last, there was true opposition to Edward, and the Scots' search for an ally drew them naturally towards France. With, hardly surprisingly, Philip the Fair being more than willing to countenance an alliance whereby England would come under threat along its northern border, a treaty was negotiated by which each country agreed to assist the other militarily in the event of an English invasion. The treaty was signed by Philip in Paris on 23rd October 1295 and by John on 23rd February 1296, in Berwick. The auld alliance had been born; henceforth Scotland and France would act against their common enemy, England, the auld enemy (except, that is, when it suited the French to treat with or have their perfidious Channel neighbour as an ally, leaving Scotland hanging out to dry).

Buoyed by this newly formed alliance, the Scots demurred when Edward demanded that Berwick and its castle be handed over to him pending the outcome of his war in France. Garrisoned by the brave men of Fife, the town repulsed Edward's first intemperate response, an English attack by sea. The king's fleet was set alight in the estuary. No quarter was given. The Tweed ablaze, not a single English footprint was planted on Scottish soil.

Success, however, is a dangerous thing. Such was the boost given to the Scots' confidence from this early, aggressive show of defiance, that their army felt free to cross the border in the west, attack Carlisle and lay waste in the usual medieval fashion to the surrounding countryside. In part this was, or at least it was intended to be, a diversionary tactic with a view to drawing Edward's attention away from the eastern march. For Edward and his mighty army had already gathered at Newcastle. It consisted of 30,000 foot and 4,000 men at arms, and was joined by the Bishop of Durham and his army – 1,000 foot and 500 horse. The target of these two armies was Berwick, and Edward was not to be diverted. After moving north to Bamburgh, the English host marched to Wark, accompanied by those Scots noblemen who had previously sworn fealty to Edward, including, and stepping on stage for the first time, our second Robert the Bruce, son of the Competitor. In the spring sunshine the army's march was thirsty work, and so, as it approached the outskirts of the village, permission was granted for a pit stop at the Big Dun Cow, the giant landlord of which was said to be of Franco-Celtic-Viking extraction, from the clan Du Verclind. Seeing the troops approach, he called to the landlady, "Quickly, Stella, this is not a day to be running out of beer. Go down to the cellar and bring up the Boddies."

After leaving Wark, Edward and his army crossed the Tweed near Coldstream; the Bishop's army crossed near Norham. Once they had again combined, the two armies marched along the riverside, stopping and setting up camp at a nunnery perhaps a mile or so outside Berwick.

Simultaneously, the English fleet reached the mouth of the river. For two days Edward waited in vain for the town to surrender. The belligerent townsfolk and garrison responded contemptuously to Edward's call to open the gates; and those guarding the quay showed the fleet equal contempt, hurling abuse and showing not a few bare arses. This show of bravado, however, was badly misplaced. The town's defences comprised a ditch, an earth rampart and miscellaneous wooden barricades. In truth, the defensive fortifications were not worth the name, and with no army of relief in sight or even commissioned, the town was all but defenceless.

There are several different accounts of the precise circumstances that led to what all the chroniclers agree was a massacre, perpetrated by Edward and aided and abetted by our second Robert and other feudally bound Scots. The most colourful, and most anti-Plantagenet, version is given by Walter Bower in his *'Scotichronicon'*. He describes it much more colourfully than I ever could. This is what he says:

> " ...the king of England attacked Berwick in person with a large body of men, and because he could not take it by force, he planned cunningly and craftily to gain his end by deception. Therefore when he had been encamped round the town for some considerable time, he made as if he wished to withdraw, and removing the tents he pretended he was going very far away; but on 29 March (Good Friday that year) immediately after daybreak, after raising the standards and war-ensigns of the Scottish army which had been deceitfully counterfeited before-hand, he approached the gates of the town. When they saw this, the Scottish defenders of the town became thoroughly elated and delighted when it was reported to them that help from their king was at hand: being unhappily deceived by this promise, like loyal subjects and unaware of the whole

*deception, they confidently opened the gates. But as soon
as the deception was revealed and the truth learnt, they
endeavoured to resist, but were at once surrounded by
enemies and, enduring attack on every side, they were
wretchedly overwhelmed by sudden onslaughts. Moreover,
when the town had been taken in this way and its citizens
had submitted, the aforesaid king of England spared no
one, whatever the age or sex, and for two days streams
of blood flowed from the bodies of the slain, for in his
tyrannous rage he ordered 7500 souls of both sexes to be
massacred. There the noble, high-spirited and vigorous
fighting men of Fife were utterly destroyed, so that mills
could be turned round by the flow of their blood. The following lines concern the taking of this town:*

*"In 1296 the belligerent town on the Tweed called
Berwick was subdued and provided booty for the English.
Alas, foul crime!
Note that this was on 29 March."*

Those who were able to fled for their lives across Magdalene Fields.
In the town, the only significant opposition came from its thirty or so
Flemish merchants, who defended their Red Hall. It had been a gift to
them from the great Alexander, which at the time of its making they
vowed to defend with their lives. And so they did, until deep into the
evening. Eventually, the merchants and their hall were consumed by
fire, the flames rising skywards, bringing to a close the town's darkest
day. The Plantagenet, and the Bruce, had done their worst.

The Scots' response to the slaughter was to reply in kind. Retribution
was exacted in cross-border incursions in both the east and west
marches. Harbottle, Corbrigg and Hexham all suffered at the hands
of the vengeful Scots. If, however, the attacks were intended to cause
Edward to hesitate, they were dismally ineffective. He barely paused

for breath. In April he despatched John de Warenne, Earl of Surrey, to Dunbar to lead the English army into battle against the numerically greater Scottish army. On the Scots' part there was what amounted to, if any was needed, an open declaration of war, when John, backed by his council of twelve, condemned Edward for his part in the events at Berwick and renounced his homage to the English king. Perhaps it was the knowledge his army was 40,000 strong, or that his country was in alliance with France, that persuaded Balliol this was the time to finally stand up to Edward. Alternatively, it may have been a case of now or never; Warenne with his army was knocking on the door of Dunbar castle; and Edward was in Berwick, poised to advance northwards. Neither man was going away. On 27th April, less than a month after Scotland's precious royal burgh of Berwick had fallen into its enemy's hands, its army took to the battlefield to obtain redress. Instead, in the space of a few short hours, it was smashed. The debacle brought to an end, almost before it had begun, any meaningful opposition to Edward's progress in his feudal colonisation of Scotland. In May, Roxburgh and Jedburgh fell. In June it was the turn of Edinburgh, after a seven day siege, followed in short order by Stirling and Perth.

And what of John, our first Balliol? He offered his surrender and that of his countrymen in early July. At Brechin castle, on 10th July, his royal arms were torn from his surcoat (a military tunic worn over armour). Hence the denigrating nickname of 'Toom Tabard', or empty surcoat. He quickly became a marginal figure, spending several years in comfortable captivity in England before retiring in 1301 to lands he held in France, where he lived out his days until his death in 1313, his heart still bitter at how he was regarded by his fellow countrymen.

With King John Balliol in the first instance ensconced in the Tower of London and the Competitor having exited our stage through death, the July surrender seemed to our second Robert an opportune time to advance his case to fill the vacancy for king of Scotland; he had, after all, been at Edward's side at the razing of Berwick, he had been loyal to the Plantagenet cause thereafter, and he was the son and successor of the Competitor, who had won silver medal in the Great Cause. But Edward was less than impressed by his vassal's submissions; with the medieval equivalent of telling him to get on his bike, the Hammer retorted that he had not taken the kingdom from one Scottish king only to hand it to another. And so, tail between his legs, our second Robert exited stage left. In 1304 he exited altogether, and thereby paved the way for the entrance of Robert number three.

As for Edward, he continued his conquering progress until he reached Elgin, from where, his mission seemingly accomplished, he returned to Berwick, summoning a parliament to be held in the town on 23rd August 1296.

It was no ordinary parliament. Rather, it was intended as the final step in the systematic subjugation of the country to Edward's and England's rule. Significant steps, not least the removal of its king to the Tower of London, had already been taken to reduce Scotland to the status of Edward's fiefdom. Add to that the removal from the country of the physical symbols of independence – the great seal (which Edward had broken into pieces and had transported to Westminster at the conclusion of the Great Cause), the Scottish regalia and the Black Rood of St Margaret (the holiest relic in Scotland) and, most significantly of all, the Stone of Destiny – and all that remained to be done was the breaking of the Scottish spirit. And that was the purpose of the Berwick parliament, where Edward was determined to secure in unequivocal terms the personal, feudal subservience of his Scottish vassals.

Like the Great Cause before it, the parliament was a grand affair. Scotland's noblemen were again present, not however on this occasion voluntarily or as representatives of what they regarded as an independent kingdom. No, they were there to pay their feudal dues, to take their oath of fealty to Edward. They promised for themselves and their heirs that they would be true, loyal and faithful to Edward and his successors: they would serve against his enemies (not least the king of

France) with life and limb. So many were there who took the oath, each and every one reduced to writing with seals applied, that the notaries recording the event required 35 skins of parchment to complete their task. The resulting document was the Ragman Roll.

Was this the end, in Berwick castle, as the nobility one by one had their names added to the Roll, the last hour of Scotland's last day as a determinedly independent people? The whole country had, it seemed, bowed down before and been broken by the Hammer, including, it should be noted, he who would one day be king of Scotland, our third Robert. But no, it wasn't the end, because there was one person on the scene missing, absent from the Berwick parliament, whose name you will not find on the Ragman Roll. In our story there is only one William with a major role to play, but one is enough, for, out of Selkirk Forest, Braveheart himself, William Wallace, was about to emerge to spark the country into its first rebellion against Plantagenet colonialism.

Chapter Five
The First Rising: Wallace Walks Like a Giant

The Wallace will make his first, dramatic, entrance very shortly but, for the moment, Edward is the only player of any significance on stage. He has achieved his aim, or so it appears. Scotland is his dominion, in which Berwick is to be the centre of government and financial administration, the capital of Scotland in England. That, in any event, is how Edward envisaged he would turn swift military success into permanent political domination.

The first step in the process of feudal colonisation was financial provision for the strengthening of the town's defences, such as they were. Funds were made available to improve and build upon the existing wooden structures (although in fact it was not until the reign of our second Edward that improvements of any substance were undertaken), and to the north of the town a ditch was cut, 80 feet wide and 40 feet deep. Ridpath describes it thus: *'It ran from the Tweed through a portion of Cow Close, a corner of Redpath's field, and thence down by an old wall in the Greenses, over the Madgdalen Fields to the sea-shore. It is called the Spades Mire'*. Have a look at the plan on page 144. You'll find the Spades Mire at the northern end of the town. A part of it runs through the grounds of the old grammar school. I used to cross it most days, on my way to and from history lessons.

Next, Edward created great offices of state for the governance of Scotland. John de Warenne he appointed as Royal Lieutenant; Sir Hugh Cressingham as Treasurer; and William Amersham as Chancellor of the

Exchequer. The royal mint was in Golden Square and an office for the assaying of silver was to be found, naturally enough, in Silver Street.

While Warenne and Cressingham were glad to bask in the prestigious light of holding high colonial office, they were less enamoured with the prospect of life in an inhospitable, unwelcoming, foreign land. They had a special dislike of the ever present cold north wind. Wimps. They should have tried being a skinny, stick-legged thirteen year old running around the town's sea cliff pitches playing football and rugby with frozen balls. Then they would have known the true meaning of cold. It is true, though, the North Sea gales blew through the town as hard and cold in the thirteenth century as they do today, foreshadowing perhaps the chilling fate Cressingham was destined to suffer at Stirling Bridge, and which Warenne would only narrowly avoid.

Third, Berwick was to be the subject of Edward's penchant for town planning. Kingston-upon-Hull, which had benefited from Edward's attention some years earlier, was to be the model. And last but not least, the Scottish survivors of the March sack were to be moved on to make way for eager English settlers. Ethnic cleansing, you see, is not by any stretch of the imagination a modern phenomenon.

When Edward returned south in August 1296 he did so confident that Scotland was well and truly under the Hammer. In truth, however, the reality was very different. Brooding resentment at the imposition of English sheriffs and clerics combined with an absolute resistance to alien rule to produce in the early spring of 1297 a series of spontaneous, uncoordinated acts of rebellion. Notwithstanding their Ragman Roll pledges, there were stirrings of rebellion within what was left of the Scottish nobility, with risings in the north-west highlands, Dumfriesshire and Clydesdale.

Enter the Wallace. Little, in fact, is known of his life before the spring of 1297. He was neither duke nor earl nor lord nor knight. In the intensely hierarchical Scotland of the late thirteenth century he was from that class of lesser men who followed, not led, their aristocratic betters. Not Wallace, however. In May 1297 he made his first, indelible, mark on Scottish history with the murder of William Heselrig, the English Sheriff of Lanark. Whether it is true the act was one of personal vengeance for the murder of his wife by Heselrig, I can't say, though it does the legend no harm to believe it was. More significantly historically, the act was a brutal, public defiance of Edward's administration in Scotland. It galvanised Scottish opposition in the south-west and made Wallace the focal point for the nascent rebellion, an alternative to the largely ineffectual Scottish nobility.

Wallace's success and growing reputation attracted allies. One of the first was Sir William Douglas, whose imprisonment after the sack of Berwick had not lasted long. In a moment of poor judgement, Edward allowed Douglas his freedom and returned his lands to him in consideration of Douglas' oath of fealty. He broke it at the first opportunity. Together, in the late spring of 1297, Wallace and Douglas led a horseback raid on Scone. Their target was William Ormseby, Edward's chief legal officer in Scotland. Learning of the approaching raid just in time, Ormseby saved his skin by fleeing from the scene. Thwarted in his main aim of having the justiciar go the same way as Heselrig Wallace may been but, nevertheless, his morale boosting message to the Scottish people was crystal clear; the English administration was vulnerable.

As for the nobility, it was the Earl of Lennox and James the Steward who sought to assume leadership of and bring focus to the rebellion. They were joined by Douglas but Wallace, either through want of an invitation or a disinclination to play second fiddle to a discredited aristocracy, stayed away. As it turned out, the nobles' rebellion passed in the blink of an eye, ending in yet another humiliating capitulation. A simple show of English force, in the form of an army under the command of Sir Henry Percy and Sir Robert Clifford arriving at Irvine in early July 1297, was all it took for the rebellion to crumble. The recent and still vivid memory of the Dunbar debacle was too fresh in their minds for Lennox and his co-rebels to contemplate facing an English army in the field.

Thus, a peace, no a surrender, was negotiated whereby the Steward and Lennox walked away unaffected on condition only that they would confirm, once again, their feudal obligations to Edward. Douglas was not so well treated. He forfeited his lands and was imprisoned, initially in Berwick castle and later in London, where death would be his punishment for the part he had played in the abortive insurrection. The aristocratic rebellion having passed without so much as a single Scottish pike or English sword having been raised in anger, Percy and Clifford led their unscathed troops back to Berwick. Their confidence was high, and why shouldn't it have been? Isolated uprisings there may have been, making parts of the kingdom ungovernable by the English administration in Berwick, but there was nothing or no one to match the English army in the field, so they thought.

Having not been present, Wallace was untainted, even assisted, by the Irvine defeat by consent. He and his followers, for they were no army at this stage, sheltered for a time in Selkirk Forest while two consequences of Irvine operated in their favour. The first was complacency. The English colonial administration, Cressingham excepted, was lulled into a false sense of security, having yet again seen off the Scottish aristocracy. The second was that the abject capitulation of the Steward and Lennox left the country crying out for new, alternative leadership. Wallace duly obliged. With an ever growing following, he led successful campaigns in Perthshire and Fife, routing the English in the process, and in early August at Dundee he joined forces with one of the few Scottish noblemen who had stood up with any degree of success to the post-Ragman Roll English administration, Andrew Murray (no, not that one), whose family held lands in Moray. By this time Cressingham at least had become convinced Wallace posed a threat that ought to be addressed. Scotland, he said in a letter of 23rd July to Edward, was ungovernable but for Berwick and Roxburghshire, and

Wallace, encamped in Selkirk Forest with willing followers, was the cause of the disturbed peace.

But if Cressingham was anxious to confront this new threat, Warenne was distinctly underwhelmed. He had spent a significant part of 1297 on his lands in England, scheming of ways to be relieved of his military responsibilities for the maintenance of Edward's colonial administration. Reluctantly, he returned to Berwick in August, where he found waiting for him the English army recently returned from Irvine. With no great enthusiasm, in early September, he led it north out of Berwick, towards Stirling, whose castle was under English control. Intelligence of Warenne's movements soon reached Wallace, who with Andrew Murray and their combined forces, moved swiftly to encamp on high ground north of the Forth at Stirling, from where the comings and goings of the English at the castle were easily observable.

The first significant step in the preliminaries leading up to the Battle of Stirling Bridge saw Lennox and the Steward, having lost out in the leadership stakes to Wallace and Murray, switch sides and re-emerge as Warenne's unlikely peace negotiators. They approached the Scots on 9th September, were given short shrift and reported their failure to Warenne the following day. They promised faithfully to join battle on the side of the English; what they didn't say was that honouring it was to be contingent upon how the wind blew on the day of battle.

In the early morning of 11th September the English army commenced its crossing of Stirling Bridge on to the north side of the river, a little too early for their leader. Warenne was still in bed. Back, therefore, the army crossed. Once washed, dressed and breakfasted, the Royal Lieutenant of Scotland eventually gave the order to re-cross, only to countermand it at the sight of Lennox and the Steward riding towards the English camp. They were coming, surely, to bring news of another Scots' surrender or, at the very least, to make good their promise to join the fight for the Plantagenet cause. No, neither. Before melting away into the autumn mist, they stayed long enough to inform Warenne that, despite repeating their best efforts at persuading Wallace to disband the assembled Scottish host (for by now it was an army), they had failed again to do so. The news did nothing to harden Warenne's resolve. Still lacking enthusiasm for the task ahead, the Royal Lieutenant sought one more time to persuade the Scots to repeat their Irvine climb down, this time by sending a small party of Dominican monks to carry his surrender invitation.

Wallace's reply was short and unequivocal: *'Tell your commander that we are not here to make peace but to do battle to defend ourselves and liberate our kingdom. Let them come on, and we shall prove this in their very beards.'* And so they did. As Warenne prevaricated, Cressingham seized the initiative. Casting off the shackles of bureaucrat, tax collector and minder of Edward's coffers for the glory of military leadership, he rode at the front of the English army as it crossed Stirling Bridge for the third time. This time there would be no turning back; there was nowhere to turn.

Wallace watched as the vanguard soldiers made their painfully slow progress across a bridge so narrow that they could cross only two abreast. Cut off from the rest of the army, which remained on the south side of the bridge, the vanguard had just about completed its crossing when the Scots descended. With nowhere to go, the English forces were slaughtered. In the mayhem, Cressingham's military career lasted no more than an hour or two, in which he experienced not the glory but the horror of battle. Targeted by the Scottish infantry, his demise came in the most brutal of fashions. As he fell in battle, his skin was cut from his body and divided into strips for distribution as trophies of war. It is said one such strip was retained by Wallace, as a sheath for his sword. Warenne, who had led from the rear, watched the carnage from the south side of the bridge. With his army in retreat he took to his horse, stopping only when he reached the safety of Berwick. And, once the battle had been lost and won, in joined Lennox and the Steward, giving chase to the retreating English stragglers.

Coincidentally, it was on a September night when, using the light from my laptop screen, I was sitting in the back garden, having a beer or two, writing about the Wallace's heroics, when Hilary, my wife, came out to remind me there is more to life than writing about Berwick. *Keith, she said, I know there is a town in north Northumberland of which you're very fond, but come a little closer and listen to what I have to say; look up into the sky, there is a yellow moon on the rise, not any old moon, a harvest moon*, and what she said reminded me of my younger days when I saw a similar sight over the Ganges.

For Wallace, victory at Stirling Bridge was intended to be only the beginning. The recovery of towns and castles in south-east Scotland was next on his agenda. His first attempt at re-taking Berwick was thwarted. The second attempt succeeded. Probably by no later than mid-October 1297, the town was once again Scottish. The castle, however, proved too well fortified, garrisoned and supplied. It remained under English control. A similar state of affairs was found in Edinburgh and Roxburgh. Quite simply, the Scots lacked the weaponry, principally siege engines, which would have enabled them to pursue effective sieges of garrisoned English held castles.

Nevertheless, the latter part of 1297 and the early months of 1298 saw the Scots in the ascendancy with Wallace, at the height of his powers, appointed as sole Guardian of the realm. Guardian that is for Balliol, in whose cause he fought, although it is more than debatable whether anyone, including Wallace, took seriously the prospect of the deposed king ever returning to the throne.

While, however, the legend of Wallace has endured down the centuries, in truth his position as leader of the Scots in their first rising against Plantagenet rule was relatively short-lived. Even as Guardian, his grip on power was never anything other than tenuous. Certainly, the country north of the Forth was under Scottish control, but the situation south of the river, in the south-east in particular, was problematical for Wallace. His ineffectiveness in ousting the English garrisons from their castle strongholds in south-east Scotland, including Berwick, was mirrored in the army of the kingdom's incursion (an invasion it was not) into northern England in late 1297. In its winter campaign it burned, plundered and murdered as it made its progress through the English border counties, achieving, however, nothing of any military significance. Newcastle and Carlisle stood firm, leaving the Scots to take their plunder from the defenceless; Ryton village (in what is now Tyne & Wear) being a prime example; after the Scots had looted it, they burnt it to the ground.

Evidence of the fragility of the Scots' ascendancy was not long in emerging. From Flanders, where he was still embroiled in his own less than glorious campaign, Edward called a York parliament for January 1298, from which there shortly followed a muster of English forces under the leadership of the ever unenthusiastic Warenne. Reluctantly, he led them into Scotland where on 12th February the town of Roxburgh was re-taken and the Scots' siege of its castle lifted. Passing through Kelso *en route*, Warenne and his army reached Berwick on 15th February, to find the town abandoned by its Scottish inhabitants in much the same way as their English counterparts had melted away in advance of Wallace's oncoming forces in the summer of 1297. The pendulum had swung again; Berwick was, after only a few short months, back under English control. The loss of these two royal burghs in such a short space of time did not augur well for Wallace or his army of the kingdom.

After the fall of Berwick, there followed a period of quiet during which time both sides prepared for a resumption of hostilities. No doubt much to his relief – as while he disliked the town immensely it was as nothing compared to the dreadful thought of losing his skin in pursuit of Wallace – Warenne was ordered by Edward to remain in Berwick pending the king's return from his Flanders campaign. Edward was unwilling to leave anything to chance; he would personally lead the summer campaign into Scotland to right the reversal suffered at

Wallace's hands at Stirling Bridge. Awaiting the king in the town were 20,000 foot soldiers and 1,500 horsemen.

Edward was back in England by mid-March. Another York parliament was followed by another muster, on this occasion in Roxburgh in mid-June. It included the majority of the Berwick troops, the town being left under the protection of a small garrison of Gascony's finest fighting men, and was very much a multi-national force of some 30,000 or so men – English, Gascon, Welsh and Irish. Indeed, its size was a problem for Edward to the extent that, in a period of inclement weather causing a temporary halting of shipped supplies of food and other necessities from Berwick, the possibility of having to disband his army before engineering a confrontation with Wallace was very real.

It was, perhaps, knowledge of Edward's predicament that gave Wallace the confidence to do battle, for he actively encouraged his foe. The two armies met at Falkirk on 22nd July 1298. It was Stirling Bridge in reverse and for the Scots defeat was quickly followed by the end of Wallace's leadership of his country. Never in any event having enjoyed the full backing of the nobility, he was soon required to resign his guardianship, which role passed into the joint hands of our third Robert Bruce (then Earl of Carrick) and John Comyn (son of the Lord of Badenoch). It will be several years before we meet these two on stage but when we do, at Greyfriars Church in Dumfries, we shall be witness to one of the most monumentally important acts in Scottish medieval history.

As for the Wallace, he became increasingly marginalised in the several years after Falkirk, and by virtue of a proclamation of a Scottish parliament at St Andrew's in 1304 he suffered the ultimate ignominy of being made an outlaw in his own land. With Scotland once again under the Hammer and the vast majority of its nobles having made their peace with him, it would only be a matter of time before Wallace was delivered into his enemy's hands, and so it was that on 3rd August 1305 he was betrayed and handed over to the English by a fellow Scot, Sir John Mentieth, Governor of Dumbarton castle.

Wallace was transported immediately to London where, on 23rd August at Westminster Hall, he was tried by a panel of three judges handpicked for the task. Only two spoke; the first read out the charges and the second passed sentence. No evidence was heard, nor was Wallace permitted to speak in his own defence. He shouted he was no traitor; he had not, after all, sworn allegiance to Edward either at the Berwick Ragman Roll parliament or on any other occasion, but no more was he allowed to say and, unsurprisingly as Edward had already determined how Wallace would die, his protest was ignored.

The sentence passed was the harshest possible – a traitor's death, and carried out forthwith. Tied to a hurdle so that the journey by itself would not kill him, Wallace was drawn by horses along a four mile route from Westminster to Smithfield, his place of execution. There he was hanged by the neck, but not until death. The hangman's rope was cut while Wallace was still living so that he could witness his own disembowelment and see his heart viscera burnt before his eyes. Only after that gruesome act was he delivered to death by decapitation.

But even that was not the end as, after he had breathed his last, his already desecrated, headless body was hacked into a further four parts. His head was Edward's trophy; it was stuck on a pike on London Bridge for all to see. The remaining parts were distributed according to the Hammer's command. One part was sent to Newcastle to enable the toon's inhabitants to celebrate the demise of a fearful enemy, and the others were transported to Perth, Stirling and Berwick, as a reminder to the Scots of the price to be paid for opposing Edward Plantagenet. More than five centuries later, in 1849, in language typical of his book as a whole, Frederick Sheldon in his 'History of Berwick-Upon-Tweed … To Which Are Added Notices of Tweedmouth, Spittal, Etc.' gave an account of the arrival of Wallace's remains in the town as if he himself had witnessed the gory event. He described it thus:

'... on Berwick bridge, the old familiar bridge of Berwick, a quarter of the hero was exposed on high. That arm whose lightest motion could have led on a thousand men to blood and blows when on its last visit to Berwick, now hung from the point of a spear, like a mass of carrion. The flesh shrivelled, and the fingers fell away, one by one, into the clear waters of the Tweed, that almost seemed to blush in the ruddy dyes of evening at this sickening exhibition of a tyrant's revenge:- those fingers, when grasping his trenchant sword, had made many a mother childless. The passengers, as they passed along the bridge, undeterred by the brown bills of the English guard, doffed their bonnets reverentially; and as they passed the house of prayer at the foot of the bridge, threw in their dole and uttered an ave for the soul of their hero. Youths who had listened many a long winter's night in breathless ecstasy to their granddam's recital of his victories, turned red and pale by turns as they clutched their unfleshed swords, glancing grimly from the remains of the slaughtered Wallace to the guards of the ferocious foe. Women, young and tender maidens, who had admired him for his chivalrous bearing and magnanimity, gushed into a flood of bewailing tears, whispering in sobbing accents a requiem for the hero's soul. Some charitable hand, more imbued with humanity than the rest, at the dead of night removed this remnant of mortality from its gibbet, and buried it in a plot of ground within the walls, on the north-east side adjoining the church. Tradition has this lonely and unconsecrated burial-place by the name of "Wallace Green".'

Not difficult, I think, to divine where Sheldon's sympathies lay. Wallace's exit from our stage in August 1305, while immensely gratifying for the Hammer, was not, however, a transformational event; by the time of his execution the first rising had already come to nought for the Scots, and such was the strength of Edward's position that he no longer intended or needed to rule Scotland through a client king. Balliol would not be returning, nor would Edward bother himself with another process or great cause. No, Scotland would be ruled as a colony, with, as planned in 1296, Berwick as the centre of colonial government and administration.

But what the Hammer didn't foresee was a second rising, and one which his own exit would prevent him from addressing.

The Giant

This big face belongs to the man. He doesn't look much like Mel Gibson, but on the other hand, Mel Gibson doesn't look much like him. This is the Wallace, Braveheart, the essence of what it is to be Scottish.

Chapter Six
The Second Rising: Better than Paradise

A murder in a church and a death from natural causes are the key events by which our new players are ushered on stage.

With Edward disinclined to appoint another client king and with there being no earthly prospect of Balliol, ensconced as he was in comfortable retirement in France, even contemplating a return to reclaim his crown, it was game on for those who within Scotland's class of nobles were willing to take risks, against Edward and each other, in a bid to fill the void. The two magnates most closely eyeing the situations vacant column were John Comyn and our third Robert Bruce. An aristocratic family of longstanding, the Comyns, more than any other of Scotland's noble houses, including the Bruces, were associated from 1296 with leading the resistance to Plantagenet imperialism, and as head of the family John 'Red' Comyn was regarded as a legitimate, strong pretender. Robert was grandson of Bruce the Competitor who lost out to Balliol when in 1292 Edward gave judgment in the Great Cause, and son of Robert Bruce who with Edward had blood on his hands from the sack of Berwick in 1296. The first and second Roberts had, to no avail, sought to rely upon Edward's benevolence in booking an inauguration trip to Scone. And, perhaps, our third Robert initially intended to adopt the same approach, for in 1301 or 1302 he had, having defected from the Wallace camp, came into Edward's peace, serving the English king as Sheriff of Lanark and Ayr.

Sheltering under the protection of the Plantagenet umbrella, Robert could play the long game; Edward was well into his sixties, an extremely old man, and so Robert could afford to wait on either the king showing favour towards him or, more likely, an opportunity arising for him to pursue his claim on the old man's death. If, however, that is how in the early years of the fourteenth century Robert contemplated the future, the reality turned out violently, murderously different.

By pre-arrangement, Robert and Red Comyn, the two rivals for the Scottish throne, met at Greyfriars Church in Dumfries on 10th February 1306. Neither the reason why the two agreed to meet, nor what passed between them in discussion, debate or argument in the sanctity of the church is known. As to the outcome, on the other hand, there is absolute certainty; Comyn died by Robert's sword, and thereby, very possibly unintentionally, Scotland's second rising against the Plantagenet scourge was set in motion.

Whether the murder, for it was nothing less, was or was not premeditated mattered little once the deed had been done; Robert had to act decisively if he was to avoid being hunted down by Comyn's kin and allies. And act he did. With the support of Robert Wishart, the influential Bishop of Glasgow, and after making secure his base in south-west Scotland, he travelled to Scone where on 26th March he was enthroned as king of Scotland, taking unilaterally that which had been denied to his grandfather by process of law and to his father for want of being sufficiently sycophantic. In a ceremony supported by a greater section of the Scottish nobility than Robert might have reasonably expected, the crown was placed on his head by Isabel, Countess of Buchan. It was an act that, at the hands of the increasingly vengeful English king, she would soon pay for dearly.

The English reaction to these sudden changing events was underway even before Robert had reached Scone. By the end of February, the power base in the south-west he had thought so secure had been diminished to such an extent by English successes that a triumphant, or indeed any, return as king was out of the question. Then, in June, a force of some 300 cavalry and 2,000 infantry moved into Scotland from Berwick. Cupar and Perth were the first to fall. On 19th June, Robert was surprised and defeated at Methven. He escaped, but only to see his cavalry also defeated, at Loch Tay. Less than three months into his reign his crown, and his family, were in peril. The King of Summer they called him, for very few believed he would still be king by winter's start. And while he was able, nominally at least, to hold on to his crown after the Methven debacle by evading the clutches of the English force and its Scottish allies, his family did not fare quite so well. Elizabeth, his wife, and Marjorie, their daughter, he placed in the care of his brother, Neil Bruce, who arranged for them to be spirited out of the country to Norway. But their desperate flight failed. The two women were captured and transported to England, where they remained until after Bannockburn. As for Neil, he was the first notable casualty of Scotland's second rising, and the first of Robert's four brothers to lose his life in the fight for independence. Falling into English hands while defending Kildrummy castle, he was swiftly dispatched to Berwick where, enduring the same awful death as the Wallace, he was hanged, drawn and quartered.

Two other women players, both captured at Methven, were marked out for especially gruesome treatment. Robert's sister, Mary, as punishment for being his sister, was incarcerated in a wooden cage hung from the battlements of Roxburgh castle. And Countess Isabella, for having had the temerity to place the crown on Robert's head at Scone, became the miserable tenant of a similar cage, hanging from the battlements of Berwick castle. The two women would hang suspended, exposed to public view and the elements, for over eight years until relief came in 1314 after the Battle of Bannockburn.

By the autumn of 1306, Robert's putative reign had stalled and was in real danger of coming to a permanent halt. His brother Neil executed and his wife and daughter in captivity in England, Robert was a man on the run, forced into hiding. To make matters worse, Edward had accepted Robert's challenge to Plantagenet colonialism with enthusiasm. Despite his advancing years – in 1306 he was 67 – the English king relished the thought of joining the chase personally.

Where Robert spent his relatively short time in exile is a matter of some debate amongst historians. It seems he was at Kintyre for a short time before sailing to one or more of the Western Isles, and certainly eventually to Ireland; places where, through family ties, alliances, or both, he could be sure of safe haven. It is thought by some that Robert sailed from the long since vanished, near mythical, south-western estuary port of Abercluish. Whether true or not, there is no doubt he spent some time in Ireland, raising funds to pay for men, including Irish mercenaries, arms and ships, and it was not long before, in early 1307, with support manifesting itself in northern Scotland, he was persuaded to return to Scotland.

It was a decision he surely regretted deeply for, although he landed safely and was soon amongst friends, two of his three remaining brothers, Thomas and Alexander, were intercepted more or less immediately upon setting foot in south-west Scotland and peremptorily executed. And Edward was on the march into Scotland. Despite his progress having been considerably slowed by the effects of dysentery, by the end of June Edward was at Carlisle, ready to stand at the head of his army and lead it once again across the border. Ready, yes; able, no. Over ten days in late June and early July only six miles were covered, and the little progress that had been made came to a shuddering, final halt on 7th July at Burgh by Sands, in Cumbria, a few miles short of the border; Edward died from dysentery in the mid-afternoon of that day.

The Hammer's exit from the stage was arguably the most significant event, certainly in English eyes, of the wars of independence. He had been the principal player, occupying centre stage, around whom supporting actors had performed. From the moment of the Maid's death, when he sniffed an opportunity to establish, directly or indirectly, overlordship of Scotland, until his last breath, Edward had a pathological desire to subdue Scotland. Even death, he intended, would not be permitted to stand in his way, for, on his deathbed he instructed his son and successor, our second Edward, to have his *'body boiled in a large cauldron until the flesh could be separated from the bones; that he would have the flesh buried, and the bones preserved, and that every time the Scots should rebel against him he would summon his people, and carry with him the bones of his father, for he believed most firmly, that as long as his bones should be carried against the Scots, those Scots would never be victorious.'* (My thanks for this to Seymour Phillips' 'Edward II'.)

The Hammer's Westminster Abbey resting place

Here you see the back, plain side of the Hammer's Westminster Abbey tomb. The long inscription on the top line – 'Edwardus Primus Scottarium Hic Est 1308 Pactum Serva' ('Here is Edward I Hammer of the Scots … Keep Faith') was added by person, or persons, unknown several centuries after his entombment. The words underneath – 'O Non Es' – were added more recently, also by author or authors unknown.

Our second Edward is, you'll not be surprised to learn, Edward II. We'll simply refer to him as Edward, however, to save having to think 'the second' every time we mention him. And we'll refer to his father as his father or the Hammer instead of either Edward or Edward I, just to be clear whom we are talking about.

Edward was proclaimed king at Carlisle on 20th July 1307. In his first formal step as king, on 4th August at Dumfries, he made Piers Gaveston, a Gascon knight and his closest friend, Earl of Cornwall. For a monarch to bestow honours on those he favoured was hardly unusual. But, in this instance, it was controversial, because Gaveston was universally detested by England's barons. Within, therefore, a month of coming to the throne Edward had introduced into his reign a degree of instability from which it would never escape; it cost him Gaveston's life, and ultimately his own.

While the Hammer's death was a tragedy for the English, it was a blessing for the Scots, the reason being that, as an effective military leader, Edward was about as far removed from his father as it was possible to be. In this, his first venture into Scotland as king, he barely tipped his toe over the border before abandoning his father's pursuit of Robert. As we've seen, he made it as far as Dumfries, that is to say a little more than twenty or so miles over the border into southwest Scotland, but not much farther. He is recorded as having visited Sanquhar in Dumfriesshire, where he joined Gaveston to celebrate the latter's newly acquired earldom, and Cumnock in Ayrshire, but by early September 1307 he had turned homewards and was back in Carlisle, and by the end of October he was at Westminster.

To a very significant extent, the relationship between Edward and his barons was similar to that between the thirteenth century bad King John and his magnates, the outcome of which in June 1215 was Magna Carta. In Edward's case, the outcome is not much remembered or celebrated, though it is no less deserving of recognition as one of the more important episodes in the history of the contest between crown and parliament for political power and control of the constitution. Briefly, in the several years from 1307 Edward, in large part as a means of seeking to keep Gaveston by his side and of avoiding civil war, acceded to his barons' demands, transferring powers to an elected body of 21 bishops, barons and earls by which they were granted the right to reform both the governance of the kingdom and the funding of the royal household.

These were the 'Ordainers', after the publication in September 1311 of a document comprising 41 clauses – the 'Ordinances' – limiting the authority of the crown and re-affirming Magna Carta. Of course, like his predecessor John, Edward in agreeing to cede power, acted out of perceived necessity, insincerely and in bad faith, writing to the Pope only two days after their publication to seek annulment of the Ordinances. We say a little but not too much more about them here, as to do them justice another chapter or two would be needed; too much, I think, of a digression. The point to bear in mind, in the context of our story, is that Edward's ability or otherwise to campaign in Scotland was linked very closely to his dealings with the Ordainers, and his fondness for staying in Berwick is explained by the fact that it is 360 miles from London, where this troublesome, not to say rebellious, group sat.

Ridpath tells us that, in 1307, Edward had monies, raised by his sheriffs in London, applied to the purchase of weapons and other military equipment to be sent to Berwick, the intended base for a fresh campaign in Scotland. The supplies comprised 12,000 weight of iron; 500 pounds of hemp-cord for ballistae; 30,000 arrows for ballistae of one foot; 12,000 arrows for those of two feet; and 2,000 feathered arrows of copper. Amongst the victuals sent north were twenty barrels of honey and a hundred barrels of wine. What, you might ask, is a ballista, the plural of which is ballistae? For the answer, turn to pages 68 and 69.

However, so ineffectual was the English king that orders he issued for a muster of troops at Carlisle in August 1308 and at Berwick after Michaelmas in 1309 were simply ignored. The barons were in no mood to commit to the furtherance of the war, leaving what English troops there were still in Scotland isolated and the north of England vulnerable to cross-border incursions by tribute and booty seeking Scots. Without military assistance, the best the north could hope for was to buy Robert off. Truces were the order of the day, the terms of which, through lack of an ability on the part of the English to enforce them, Robert observed or ignored as he pleased. Edward's inability to furnish meaningful military assistance was such that, in December 1309, all he could do to support the garrisons at Perth, Ayr, Banff and Dundee was to encourage them to negotiate local truces on the best terms available to them. Subsequently, a general truce was negotiated to last to June 1310. Save that the north of England was temporarily spared the trauma of having to suffer further Scottish raids, the party who benefited most from the truce was Robert, who by virtue of the cessation of hostilities was allowed yet more time to strengthen his position.

Edward, at last, in 1310, found himself in a position to venture northwards, with moderate support from the barons, who now had at least two reasons to back their monarch. Firstly, they realised not only was Scotland in danger of becoming a completely lost cause but also that there was a real risk of the border in the eastern march creeping southwards to encompass Berwick and more. Secondly, notwithstanding Gaveston remained an intense irritation to them, the Ordainers had otherwise achieved much; their 21 elected representatives were in place and draft Ordinances had been prepared and were proceeding, slowly, towards publication.

For Edward, conveniently, the forthcoming campaign would enable him to put as much geographical distance as possible between the Ordainers and himself, thereby, he hoped, putting the brakes on any further moves towards publication of the Ordinances. As an added bonus Gaveston happened to be in Perth. In September, 3,000 mainly Welsh infantry descended on Berwick in readiness for Edward leading them into Scotland. Leaving the town under the protection of its standing garrison, and supplemented by 100 crossbowmen financed by the city of London, finally, over three years into his reign, Edward, via Wark, embarked on his first Scottish campaign.

In those three years, circumstances in Scotland had, however, changed markedly. Robert was no longer a fox on the run. If the parts of the south and most of south-east of Scotland were still in English hands – the castles of Dunbar, Edinburgh, Roxburgh, Stirling, Jedburgh and of course Berwick were still firmly in Edward's possession – the rest of the country had fallen under Robert's spell: an administration was in place for the collection of taxes; military service could be both required and enforced; increasing numbers of Scots had been persuaded to follow his cause; and those who had no taste for a Bruce king had been marginalised, often by having their lands taken from them.

As it turned out, Edward's campaign was a complete non-event. Robert could not be tempted into pitched battle – he stayed very firmly in the north – and so, after aimlessly wandering around the Scottish lowlands for a month or two, Edward and his troops traipsed homeward. They were back in Berwick by early November. At least setting up residence 360 odd miles from the capital would, Edward thought, have the obvious benefit of keeping him out of the reach of his troublesome barons. And so he settled himself in the town with his queen and friendly nobles, placing Gaveston, for his own safety, in nearby Bamburgh castle. To maintain the appearance of being in Berwick for reasons other than avoiding his London troubles, Edward ventured once more into Scotland in March 1311. With Robert nowhere to be found, the English king returned to Berwick with nothing to show for his limited, unenthusiastic attempt to engage the opposition.

As attractive as the prospect surely was (after all, who could resist the town's charms?), Edward could not holiday in Berwick indefinitely. London called. The Ordainers were determined to see the Ordinances published, and the barons were more hostile than ever towards Gaveston. If Edward was to avoid civil war he would have no choice but to return south, and this he duly did, departing in July 1311 and arriving in London on 11th August. Parliament met soon afterwards and, finally, on 29th September, the Ordinances were published. Among the concessions made by Edward in the process were that Gaveston would be sent into permanent exile (again) and Edward would not recommence the war against the Scots or leave England without the permission of the barons in parliament. Regarding the first of these concessions, as we shall shortly see, Edward had no intention of adhering to it.

By returning to London after his prolonged stay in Berwick and by appearing, however insincerely, to accede to the Ordainers' demands, Edward averted civil war, for which the north of England paid the price, with Robert and his army free to conduct unopposed cross-border raids, firstly in the west through Solway for eight days from 12th August, and subsequently through Northumberland for two weeks from 8th September. Haltwhistle, Harbottle, Holystone, Redesdale and Corbridge were all devastated in these raids as the Scots gathered in livestock, food supplies and what other booty they could lay their hands on to take back across the border. What they couldn't take with them they burned.

English in-fighting continued well into 1312, culminating in Gaveston falling into the hands of Edward's opponents in May and his execution in June, with the Earls of Lancaster, Warwick, Hereford and Arundel being complicit.

In the chaos and paralysis that marked governance in England at this time, Robert remained free to terrorise the north of the country. Hexham, Corbridge, Durham and Hartlepool were targeted in August 1312. Norham, too, burned. Defenceless, and without hope of receiving military assistance, the northern counties could hope to avoid complete devastation only by buying Robert off with money tributes in return for truces. The Bishopric of Durham and the counties of Northumberland, Westmoreland and Cumberland all put monies into Robert's war chest.

On 6th December 1312 Robert made his first attempt at wresting Berwick back for Scotland. A night attack; rope ladders used to scale the walls; but down the road a dog was barking; the garrison was alerted and the attempt thwarted. But if the town could for the time being be defended, many of Edward's strongholds in Scotland were much more vulnerable. Perth was the first to fall, in January 1313; Roxburgh and Dumfries followed in February. The capture in March of Edinburgh castle by the Scots left Edward with only Stirling and Berwick. In the early months of 1314, Stirling castle came under immense pressure from Robert's sole surviving brother (inevitably an Edward just to confuse us). With a significant force, Edward had laid siege to the castle, and its governor, Sir Philip Mowbray, had undertaken to surrender it if by Midsummer's Day (24th June) 1314 the siege had not been lifted.

The clock towards Bannockburn was well and truly ticking. And this time the barons and earls of England, fearing still the north of the country as well as Scotland could be lost permanently to Robert, were willing to support their king. Throughout May and the first week of June 1314, Berwick witnessed the arrival of thousands of English and Welsh infantrymen, joined by a plethora of barons, earls, knights and men-at-arms. The only notable absentees from the ranks of the aristocracy were the Earls of Lancaster, Warwick, Arundel and Surrey. At last, seven years into his reign, Edward had amassed an army to rival any his father had been able to summon and, on 11th June, he arrived in Berwick ready to lead it into battle. Ridpath tells us that on the sixth or seventh day before Midsummer's Day Edward was at the head of an army over 100,000 strong as it started moving north towards Stirling. A more accurate estimate of the army's size is perhaps 20,000–25,000. Whatever its true size, there is no doubt it was a much more substantial force than that waiting for it under Robert's command – he had at his disposal 5,000–6,000 infantry and 500 light cavalry.

Edward and his army reached Stirling on 23rd June. Immediately upon doing so, without rest or recuperation, two divisions of his cavalry recklessly raced into action. The first, led by a knight, Henry de Bouhn, entered the forest area, New Park, where they believed they would be able to flush out the retreating Scots infantry. As they advanced, a contour dip by Pear Hill confused them into believing they were approaching a vacated broad clearing. To their surprise, what they found instead was a sizeable opposing force, led by none other than the Scottish king. De Bouhn, seeking to seize the moment and become a national hero – by killing their king the Scottish army would melt way and the siege would be lifted – challenged Robert to single combat. Robert accepted. De Bouhn charged with his lance, missed, and was decapitated by a single blow from Robert's battle-axe. This was hardly a promising start to the hostilities for the English, and it did not get any better when their second cavalry attack, a direct assault on the castle without support from either infantry or archers, was easily repulsed.

It was quite possible, on Midsummer's Eve, for the confrontation to have ended with those two skirmishes, for neither Edward nor Robert was yet committed to open battle. What persuaded Edward to proceed was pride and, ultimately misplaced, confidence that his army of aristocratic horsemen would easily overrun the spear-holding Scottish infantry. Long into the night, Edward's military commanders counselled against doing battle; after a march of 50 miles, rest was needed. Edward demurred. His cavalry would win the day and Stirling castle would be relieved. In the Scots' camp, Robert knew the risks of confronting a numerically superior and better equipped force. Defeat would mean the end of his reign, not to mention the likely annihilation of his army. He was initially minded to avoid battle by adopting the tried and tested practice of having his army drift away in the night. His mind was changed by Sir Alexander Seton, a Scottish knight previously loyal to Edward but who during the night defected and reported to Robert the low morale of the English forces and the disagreements between Edward and his military advisers.

If only Edward had heeded the wise counsel of his commanders; if only, perhaps, he had carried with him his father's bones and thrust them at the rebellious Scots, the outcome of the Battle of Bannockburn might have been different. But he did neither, and the result was defeat and humiliation, celebrated still by Scots upon every rendition and in every verse of *Flower of Scotland*, when we're reminded Edward was 'senet hamewart tae think again', via Dunbar castle and from there by sea to Bamburgh and then Berwick. He arrived in the town on 27th June. Awaiting him to offer comfort and solace was his queen, Isabella. Over the ensuing several days he was joined by what survived of his army. Tempting though it undoubtedly was, as a refuge more from his enemies and critics in England than the Scottish forces on the other side of the border, Edward could not afford to linger long in the town. He therefore headed south, to York, on 9th July, his principal concern being yet again to avoid civil war.

As for the Scots, in the immediate aftermath of the battle they enjoyed the spoils of victory. Stirling castle, money, military equipment and, for ransom, aristocratic hostages by the dozen fell into their hands. Robert, offering the earl of Hereford in exchange, was at last able to secure the release of his queen, Elizabeth de Burgh, and their daughter, Marjorie. The caged Mary at Roxburgh and Isabella at Berwick also, mercifully, were given their freedom. Northern England remained defenceless, and by early August had endured its first post-Bannockburn raid. The raiding party, led by Edward Bruce, crossed the Tweed at Norham and then rampaged through Northumberland and its neighbouring counties, venturing as far south as Swaledale. It was the first of many such raids until Robert put a stop to them in 1322.

Despite some lingering allegiance to Edward amongst a small section of the nobility, Scotland was free from Plantagenet influence. Two matters, however, remained outstanding; recognition of the country's independence and the recovery of Berwick. A short poem for you regarding Robert's dominion, courtesy of Ridpath:

Fra the Red Swyr unto Orkney
was nought of Scotland fra his say
outaken Berwick it alone.

I'm sure you get the gist. A rough translation is:

From the Red Swyr to Orkney
all Scotland was subject to him
except for Berwick.

Where, I hear you ask, is the Red Swyr? Google tells me it might have been a place in Galloway or possibly a section of Roman road near the Tyne, but other than that I have no idea.

Edward was certainly fearful the town would be lost. He therefore ensured its defences were strengthened, its garrison maintained and that it received generous supplies of wheat and oats. That he was prepared to take such measures while simultaneously abandoning most of the rest of northern England to suffer the interminable misery inflicted by cross-border raiding parties is an indication of Berwick's importance to Edward, and by the same token of its importance to Scotland. He was determined not to allow it to fall into Robert's hands; instead it would once again be the gathering point for an army of invasion, for Edward, humiliated though he had been, did not regard Bannockburn as anything more than a temporary setback. Having no intention of acceding to Robert's demand to be recognised as king of an independent Scotland, Edward was in Berwick again in June 1315 seeking to raise an army for yet another expedition into Scotland. He issued a summons for an army to gather at Newcastle on 15th August, from where it would march to Berwick and then across the border in search of revenge for Bannockburn. At least that was Edward's plan, but it proved to be hopelessly fanciful, because, such was the weakness of his position in England, that acting in unison the barons, on whom he was dependent for providing his army, simply ignored the summons. Edward was forced homeward once more, this time without even setting foot in Scotland. He could find comfort only in the knowledge that an attempt by the Scots to recover the town by sea had been swiftly and easily repulsed.

What Edward could not achieve militarily he endeavoured to secure through diplomacy. By sending a delegation to Avignon, he persuaded the recently elected Pope John XXII in 1317 to issue a papal bull requiring Robert to observe a two year truce with England, on pain of excommunication if the Scottish king ignored the command. Communications were rather slower in the fourteenth century than in these modern times. It was not until several months later, in December 1317, that an attempt was made to deliver the bull to Robert. The task fell to one Adam Newton, a Berwick Minorite friar. Adam didn't have far to travel. He found Robert and his forces near Old Cambus, just off the A1 (not that the A1 was around at the time) north-east of Grantshouse, twenty or so miles from Berwick, preparing for an assault on the town. Nor was he treated well by Robert, who refused even to allow him into his presence. The message to Adam was unequivocal: there would be no truce, even on pain of excommunication, until he was acknowledged as king of Scotland and, equally importantly, Berwick was delivered back to Scotland.

Excommunication – eternal damnation – was a price worth paying for Robert and for his right hand man, James Douglas. Such was the importance of the town to them that both were willing to defy the Pope's instruction to make peace with England. Robert insisted he "would have Berwick", and for his part Douglas exclaimed he would rather enter Berwick than the gates of Paradise. Berwick better than Paradise? Now there's a thought.

When I was a boy I was convinced that one day I would enter paradise on earth, Celtic Park. On the Oval, the Billendean, the Five Arches, the Playing Fields, and the Stanks (of which more later), and not forgetting my time as a ball boy at Shielfield Park, I honed my footballing skills to such a degree that, to my mind, the only question was whether, with my sweet left foot, I'd be the next Bertie Auld or, with my keen reflexes and salmon-like agility (what else for a boy born on the north bank of the Tweed?), the next Ronnie Simpson. I was going to be, and still will be, a Lisbon Ryan.

Back to the business in hand. Despite the setback, in the absence of a viable military alternative, Edward still hoped for a diplomatic settlement. Robert played along. In early 1318, the two kings agreed to the appointment of eight Vatican authorised commissioners charged with the task of negotiating a settlement and who were to commence their work in Berwick. They never did start. On 2nd April 1318, before the commissioners were anywhere near the town, back into Scotland's hands it fell.

There was no long siege, no pitched battle, just a little skulduggery, treachery and, perhaps, bribery. The English chroniclers' account is that the town's governor, Peter Spalding, sold it to Robert for an unspecified but no doubt generous sum of money. In the Scottish version of events the same Peter Spalding, as a burgess of the town, not governor, acts out of a sense of moral imperative, not for anything as sinful as 30 pieces of silver. It was, say the Scottish chroniclers, Peter's wish to free the Scottish inhabitants of the town from the cruelty shown towards them by its English governor that caused him to act. Either way, out came the scaling ladders for a second time, Peter having arranged, on a night when he was on watch duty, to allow a Scots contingent – men of Lothian all – to enter through Cowport. Stealthily, they made their way past the Bell Tower and the Greenses, pausing only for a pint in the Pilot, to Cowport. On this occasion there was no barking dog to alert the garrison, only Spalding on hand to allow them entry into the town. When daylight broke a bloody battle commenced. The men of Lothian, it seems, were in the first instance more concerned with what plunder they could lay their hands on than on securing the town and, consequently, lost the advantage gained by their surprise attack. Eventually, however they prevailed: the garrison was driven back into the castle. Six days later the castle fell. To the chimes of freedom flashing, Robert entered the town the following day, proclaiming this is our patch of ground, people. As Sheldon puts it, referring to the Competitor and the rejection of his claim to the Scottish crown in the Great Cause:

> *'Little did [Robert's] grandfather imagine, when he sued for the throne of Scotland in that very hall, that a grandson of his should revive the fallen glories of Scotland, and dictate to the son of that king who denied him his claim.'*

Scotland was whole again. Robert and Douglas were duly excommunicated. When the victorious Scottish king was given the news he railed against it. My medieval Scottish isn't that good, so, in my best *Sunday Post* accent, this is his plea to his maker in the modern vernacular: *"Mark, God, dinna forsake us, yer wee Rab and his pal, Jamie. Jings! Berwick's a braw toon, and it wiz oors in the first place."*

Chapter Seven
Independence Day

With Berwick safely back in Scotland's possession, all that remained for Robert to achieve was acknowledgement of the kingdom's independence by those outside its borders. When it suited their interests, the Scots were just as willing as the English to call on the good offices of the Pope and, sure enough, it was to Pope John XXII they turned in 1320 with a plea that he recognise the country's right to exist free from English subjugation or interference. This was the Declaration of Arbroath. It begins with a direct reference to the Hammer's diplomatic manoeuvrings in the Great Cause and his subsequent prolonged military assaults, which began of course with the sack of Berwick:

> *'Thus...our nation did indeed live in freedom and peace up to the time when that mighty prince the King of the English, Edward, the father of the one who reigns today, when our kingdom had no head and our people harboured no malice or treachery and were then unused to wars or invasions, came in the guise of a friend and ally to harass them as an enemy.'*

It is then followed by as eloquent an assertion of nationhood and national identity as can be found anywhere:

*'... for, as long as but a hundred of us remain alive, never
will we on any conditions be brought under English rule.
It is in truth not for glory, nor riches, nor honours that we
are fighting, but for freedom – for that alone, which no
honest man gives up but with life itself.'*

It would be some years later, however, before the prize – independence in the eyes of others – would be won, and once won it was very soon afterwards put under grave threat.

In the meantime, Robert turned his attention to the defence of Berwick. He resolved to maintain a strong garrison presence and strengthen its walls, for which he appointed a team of engineers led by a Flemish knight, Sir John Crabb. It wasn't long before the improvements made were put to the test. The loss of Berwick was just the latest in a long line of personal humiliations for Edward. By failing to retain it he had lost the jewel stolen by his father, and what was to have been the centre for English governmental and administrative rule in Scotland was now a Scottish first line of defence in the east and, worse still, a base for launching raids into Northumberland and other counties of north-eastern England. Winning the town back was a must for Edward.

The year 1319 was one of the few in Edward's unhappy reign when he wasn't in perilous dispute with his aristocratic vassals. For once, more perhaps because the nobility were more fearful of suffering permanent losses of northern lands to the Scots than through any feelings of loyalty to their king, there was, almost, unanimity. Another Scottish campaign was required, and the re-taking of Berwick was an imperative first step.

Such was the degree of consensus that Edward was able to raise significant sums in taxation, from the citizenry and clergy alike, allowing him to muster an army of invasion not much smaller than his Bannockburn host. Having travelled through central England and the counties of the north-east, he and his army arrived outside the town walls on 1st September. It included an impressive array of English noblemen; including the Earls of Lancaster, Pembroke, Arundel, and Hertford; and a Scotsman, one Edward Balliol, son of the late King John of the Great Cause and, but for Robert the Usurper, the rightful king of Scotland in the eyes of those who remained loyal to the Balliol cause. He plays only a bit part in the siege but that is not by any means the last we see of him.

Also present at Berwick, at the mouth of the Tweed, was a fleet of 77 ships, sent from England's Cinque Ports (that is to say Hastings, New Romney, Hythe, Dover, and Sandwich) to lend support to the siege and prevent the supply of the town by sea. And still there was more, in the form of an army of mercenaries, willing to serve on the side of the English in reliance on Edward's promise that each and every one of them would, on the town falling, be entitled to retain for themselves £100 of booty extracted from their Scottish victims. An early example of a 'no win, no fee' agreement?

Whatever works had been undertaken in the year or so Berwick had been in Scottish hands must have been rather modest in scale, as:

> *'The walls of the town were*
> *so low, that a man with a spear,*
> *might strike another upon the face.'*

The town was vulnerable. The first assault was made on 7th September. It was, inevitably, a bloody affair. A short Greek lesson for you. A feature of medieval warfare was the siege engine, of which there were many forms, the purpose of which was to pummel defensive fortifications and the enemy into submission. In this first assault, the English forces relied on two such devices, the catapaulta and the ballista. Now for the lesson: deriving from the Greek 'Katpeltes', meaning shield piercer, the catapaulta was a machine for hurling javelins and shooting arrows at such high velocity that armour and shield provided no defence; the ballista, from the Greek 'ballistes', meaning to throw, was essentially a giant crossbow designed to fire enormous bolt darts along a low, flat trajectory – a single dart was capable of skewering several of the enemy at the same time. Add to those devices a trebuchet or two and a battering ram so large that it took 50 men to lift it, once the assault was underway it was going to be a long day for the Scots. To defend themselves, they at least had the advantage of being able to look down upon the enemy as it was the turn of the English to climb the scaling ladders. Stones, rocks and scalding water were applied in keeping the English at bay. The besiegers, however, had a trick up their collective sleeve, which presumably someone thought was a stroke of genius, and dispensed with the need for climbing ladders. When the tide was at its highest point, an English ship approached and came to rest against the riverside walls. On top of the ship's mast was affixed a boat and in the boat was a contingent of sailors supplied with a ladder which they planned to lay horizontally between the mast and the top of the wall. Once the ladder was in place they would cross it and enter the town. This, alas, was one of those ingenious plans that, when put into practice, does not unfold in quite the manner envisaged. Not a single sailor made it across to the wall. The Scots, with shot, stones, bolts, arrows and spears, easily repelled their foe. Those who managed to make it back across the ladder bridge, surely much to their chagrin, discovered that in the ebbing tide their ship was stuck fast aground on the river bed. Slaughter followed as the Scots set the ship alight.

Despite the first assault ending in failure, Edward was hardly deterred, and had good reason for believing it was only a matter of time before the besieged town would be surrendered to him. He ordered a second assault on 13th September, with a new siege engine introduced into the fray. No Greek lesson needed this time. It was a sow, though it didn't look much like one. Picture a gigantic wardrobe on wheels and divided into compartments. The top compartment housed men who, like the courageous sailors of the first assault, intended to enter the town by a ladder bridge over the top of the walls. On the floor of the wardrobe were miners whose task it was to dig away at the foundations of the walls, causing them to crumble and collapse. Another genius idea was about to bite the dust. How good an engineer Sir John Crabb was is not recorded, but he was, it seems, a man of enormous strength as, single-handedly, he is said to have picked up a boulder of immense dimensions and hurled it from the walls on to the roof of the sow, causing it to split asunder.

The main land thrust of this second English attack was directed at Scotsgate. While it was repulsed, as was a simultaneous assault by the English fleet, it hardly seemed to matter; the Scots were exhausted and the English, with such superior numbers, merely retired to Tweedmouth to regroup and prepare for a third assault.

Where, you have been asking, is Robert's army? Surely it will come charging down the A1 to rescue the town for which he was willing to be cast into the fires of Hell? Well, appear it certainly did, but not down the A1, for, as Edward and his army were marching north through the eastern English counties, the Scottish army entered England in the north-west and then, with the English army safely out of the way in north Northumberland, it crossed eastwards to set up camp on the bonnie, bonnie banks of the River Swale at Myton, about ten miles from York. This was not a very happy state of affairs for the good people of the city, whose fighting men were sitting on the banks of another river, the Tweed, 150 miles north of where they were now needed. Courageously, if foolhardily, the citizenry, peasantry and clergy of the city seized the initiative. A people's force was mustered and, employing the well-known adage that attack is the best form of defence, it marched out through the city gates on 12th September to surprise the Scots in their camp. Predictably, inevitably, surprise was no substitute for skill and experience in battle. The Scots prevailed, largely without loss.

News of the Myton debacle, which left York defenceless, reached the English camp at Tweedmouth on 13th September, in the evening of the second failed attempt to re-take Berwick. The immediate reaction of the mighty English barons was one of panic and, human nature being what it is, and the instinct for self-preservation triumphing over any notion of loyalty to others, the northern lords withdrew from the siege – one might even say deserted – to protect their lands, leaving a beleaguered Edward with only a rump of an army that had no prospect of taking the town, let alone pursuing a military campaign in Scotland. Thwarted and humiliated militarily once again, the English king abandoned the siege on 17th September, never again to return to Berwick. The town, for the time being, remained safe in Scottish hands. And York was equally safe in English hands, unmolested by the Scots after Myton, notwithstanding the city had been ripe for plundering.

And so, for poor Edward, it was not to be. Even from a position of such overwhelming strength, he had been unable to recover the jewel. And if that were not bad enough, the chaos of his reign in England showed no signs of abating, with civil war ensuing in 1321. He survived the rebellion, and was sufficiently deluded by his success to seek one more time to make Scotland his. He led an army larger even than his Bannockburn host into Lothian in the summer of 1322, bypassing the stubbornly awkward border town of Berwick on the way, only to complain that he couldn't find 'man nor beast', Robert thwarting his opponent by keeping his army in the north. The campaign, which was to be Edward's last, petered out without even a skirmish deserving of the name.

If Edward could not have Scotland, neither was he willing to give it up to Robert. And Robert, for all his success, knew that his army could never inflict a decisive military defeat over Edward on English soil. For both men, then, a thirteen year truce, confirmed by Robert from Berwick in May 1323, was an acceptable, if unpalatable, compromise. The truce held out the prospect, sadly unrealised, that the communities of northern England would be free from the plague of Scottish raids and payment of protection monies from their ever depleting coffers, and, for the people of Berwick, some respite after seventeen years of almost continuous warfare. Sheldon is surely right when he says that the people of the town were exhausted and had reached the point where they cared little about whether the town was in English or Scottish hands as, whichever it was, they were the ones from whom monies were extracted to pay for the town's defences. He suggests you read *Aesop's Fables*, in particular one about the ass and the old shepherd.

The peace benefited Robert. He was able to further strengthen his position in Scotland, which was enhanced in May 1324 with the birth of a son and heir, David. Robert could at last see the future; a Bruce dynasty to rival the House of Dunkeld was in the making. Even the French were helping. The king of France, Charles IV, recognised Robert as the rightful king of Scotland, and in 1326 new life was breathed into the auld alliance by the Treaty of Corbeil under the terms of which, in the typical inequality of obligations that characterised the alliance in its various guises over the centuries, Scotland promised to provide military assistance to France in the event of a Franco-English war, whereas, in any war between the auld enemies, France was obliged to furnish its junior ally merely with aid and assistance. That, however, was enough for Robert. Recognition of independence by an alliance, albeit one-sided, with the most powerful kingdom in Europe, could do nothing but lend legitimacy to his rule.

The year 1326 was probably about the time, if the thought had not occurred to him before, that Edward wished he had been born a humble vassal, a peasant farmer living a peaceful, anonymous life, in a quiet English countryside hamlet, with a loyal wife, loving children and good friends. But that was not the life Edward lived. In 1325 he had the galling, some might say gauling, experience of seeing his queen, Isabella, leave him to set up camp in France with her lover, Roger Mortimer, one of Edward's many magnate enemies. And now, in September 1326, the two returned to England to wage civil war against him. It was over almost before it had started. In the simplistic, unsympathetic, cynical language of the twenty first century, Edward had lost it; his kingdom and his mind. He was captured in November, ironically on his way to Scotland, where he hoped to form an alliance with Robert. He was going to offer a deal; in return for Scottish assistance in attacking his enemies in England he would recognise Robert as king of an independent Scotland. Would Robert have accepted? We'll never know.

In January 1327, two months after his capture, Edward was deposed and not long afterwards, at Mortimer's instigation, brutally murdered. As for his reign, it is no exaggeration to say it was, from an English perspective, a miserable, unmitigated disaster. From beginning to end he was in dispute with his barons, predominantly over his propensity for favouring friends of dubious qualities; and everything his father had achieved in Scotland was lost.

For the northern English counties, Edward's troubles meant the thirteen year truce negotiated in 1323 was no truce at all. Robert, knowing the civil war in England left the north of the country exposed and defenceless yet again, sanctioned a resumption of cross-border raids including, this time around, ferocious, though unsuccessful, assaults on the castles of Alnwick, Dunstanburgh, and Carlisle. And, on the very day our next player steps tentatively on stage for the first time, Robert's forces, in a consciously public demonstration of where power resides in the borders, unleash a fearsome attack on one of England's most strategically important and heavily defended military bases, Norham castle.

Our new stage entrant is Edward's sixteen year old son, and yet another Edward, Edward III, the new king of England (so, remember, from this point onwards, this is the Edward we are talking about, unless we mean Edward Balliol of Scotland, and until we meet our next Edward, who, surprise surprise, is Edward IV).

You might have thought that the first thing on the mind of a newly crowned teenage king, having come to the throne in less than glorious circumstances, and supported by the most unstable of regencies in the persons of his mother, Isabella, and her lover, Roger Mortimer, would be to secure his own position. Not a bit of it. With all the bravado and foolhardiness of youth, Edward wasted no time in planning and launching a campaign against the Scots. He saw himself as his grandfather's grandson, not his father's son, if you know what I mean, not that you would have thought it from this first kingly venture, when he didn't even make it across the border.

Embarrassingly, almost fatally, near Stanhope Park in north-east England his army couldn't find their enemy until, in a surprise night attack, the Scots found them, turning up in the English camp and coming within a whisker of capturing Edward. It was all too much for the newly crowned king, who wept youthful tears of failure, believing that the footsteps he was destined to follow were, after all, those of his father. He needn't, however, have worried. His day as warrior king was coming despite, in the short term, having to bide his time as Isabella and Mortimer treated with the Scots. Power in England was a sufficient aphrodisiac for the regents; for them Scotland was an irrelevance. Negotiations for peace commenced in October 1327. Agreed heads of terms quickly followed. The full terms were agreed in Edinburgh on 17th March 1328, ratified in Northampton by Edward, through gritted teeth, on 4th May, and made effective retrospectively from 1st March. Independence Day. These were the main terms of the treaty:

1. Edward gave up all rights to the throne of Scotland and recognised Robert as the nation's rightful king.

2. Scotland would pay to England as compensation for damage inflicted during the wars of independence a sum of £20,000. The sum was to be paid in three annual instalments, each of which was to be handed over ceremoniously by the Scots to the English in that most English of places, Tweedmouth, outside the Harrow. It was a term the Scots complied with in full.

3. To cement this newly found accord there would be a royal marriage between Robert's son, David, and Edward's sister, Joan, and, symbolically, the wedding ceremony would be held in Berwick.
4. The Stone of Destiny would be returned to Scone. It arrived in Edinburgh on 30th November 1996, a mere 668 years late.

The wedding was held on 17th July 1328. Joan was a mere seven years old. David was even younger. At the grand old age of three, he wasn't even present at the ceremony. Absent on the ground he was 'sick', the young David was married by proxy, represented at the wedding – to emphasise no doubt the certainty of what was going to be a perpetual peace between the two nations – by Robert's two most fearsome military lieutenants, the Earls of Murray and Douglas. Joan, poor girl, was present, her purpose in life determined for her at such a young age by the exigencies of royal politics. She was to be the symbol of the new relationship between the former warring parties – she was Joan 'Make Peace'. If Sheldon were with us today he would be a racing certainty for the position of the BBC's royal correspondent. This is how he describes the wedding day:

> '... the burghers of Berwick were all alive with glee and happiness. A wedding party were on their way to Berwick. The town still showed grim signs of its late warfare; flowers in festoons hung over the blood-stained walls; the houses were hung with flags and scarfs like a gay bridegroom; burgesses and yeoman went about in their holiday attire; the town was in an uproar of merriment; old men were seen pledging each other with cups of wine, and recounting the perilous sieges of the first and second Edwards... Amid a flourish of trumpets, bugles, mynstrels' chorus, and the shouts of the populace, Joan, the youngest sister of

Edward III, the valorous daughter of the deposed mon-
arch, passed into Berwick... Tapestry and webs of scarlet
cloth were spread in the road for the Princess to travel
upon; here and there she bowed her young and beautiful
head, arching her swan-like neck as she acknowledged the
courtesies of the populace.'

Joan's dowry was the return into Scotland's possession of the Ragman Roll, the document by which so many Scottish nobles had in 1296 surrendered their independence. All was sweetness, harmony and light, but not for long.

Robert enjoyed the fruits of success, having, in the 22 years from his murderous act in the sanctity of Greyfriars Church in Dumfries, completed in full his journey from usurper to legitimate and rightful king of Scotland, for only a very short period of time. On 7th June 1329 he died, of leprosy. In the same month his excommunication was lifted. Another exit. And like his arch foe, the first Edward, on his death bed Robert left a command – that battle in open warfare against the English be avoided at all costs. And, just as his enemy's injunction was ignored, so was Robert's. His son and heir David, now king and married at five years old, can safely be said not to have been the direct recipient of his father's injunction, and so it fell to his guardians to heed Robert's words.

As it turned out, being David's guardian was something of a poisoned chalice. Of the five men who held the post in the four years from 1329 to 1333, four went to meet their maker and the fifth spent time at his majesty's pleasure in England. The first of the guardians was Robert's trusted right hand man and fellow former ex-communicant, James Douglas. It appears it did not occur to Douglas that keeping the boy king close to him was his foremost duty as he promptly set off on a pilgrimage to the Holy Land, having charged himself with the task of delivering Robert's heart, which he kept in a silver casket, to the

Church of the Holy Sepulchre in Jerusalem. His journey, and his guardianship, ended prematurely in death in a skirmish in Spain. Robert's heart was saved but never delivered to its intended destination. Melrose Abbey in the Scottish borders is its final resting place. We'll meet the remaining four guardians in the next chapter.

And if Robert, alas, did not long survive the signing of the Treaty of Edinburgh Northampton, it was also the case that the treaty did not long survive him. By the early 1330s an Anglo-Scottish war was again in the air.

In the autumn of 1330, Edward, at the still youthful age of nineteen, turned from boy to man. In a daring raid on Nottingham castle, he and a small number of trusted companions seized Mortimer, who was shortly afterwards summarily dealt with. The regency had come to an end as violently and abruptly as it had come into being. Edward was now king in the true sense, and was determined to take his place centre stage. Berwick was to be that stage.

Chapter Eight
O Folly of Scotland

Let's pause for a moment or two to remind ourselves of who is who. All the principal players in the early part of our drama have, through death, left the stage. Two English kings, the first two Edwards, have departed together with two Scottish kings, John Balliol of the Great Cause and Robert Bruce, the saviour of Scotland's independence. The Wallace has gone in life but not in spirit, his remains watching on defiantly from his Berwick resting place.

On to the stage have stepped three sons: Edward of England, son of Edward II; Edward of Scotland, son of John Balliol; and young David, Robert's son. The two Edwards (the Scottish one we shall refer to as 'Balliol' so that we can tell them apart) have a certain mutuality of interests. Edward of England is intent on becoming a warrior king. While, on the one hand, he has no particular desire to have the Scottish crown for himself – he has much bigger fish to fry – now that he has turned from boy to man he is, on the other hand, determined to avenge his father's Bannockburn and other Scottish humiliations as well as his own ignominious Stanhope Park reversal. Balliol is also in vengeful, and aspirational, mood. He does want the Scottish crown, and if it means entering into unholy alliance with the grandson of the man who removed his father, John, from the throne then so be it. Indeed, the two men had started scheming even before the Nottingham castle coup, Edward having granted Balliol and his band of Disinherited followers safe passage from France to England.

In Scotland, David is under the protection of guardian number two, James Randolph. Unable to solve the thorny problem of the Disinherited, despite talks in Berwick in March 1331, as a first step in preparing for the defence of his country, Randolph oversaw improvements to the town's defences. He died, however, an untimely death in July 1332, before the awaited invasion from the south commenced. Enter guardian number three; Donald, Earl of Mar, though not for long. In August 1332, less than a month after Mar's appointment, Balliol made his move. With a relatively modest force of between 2,000 and 3,000 men, he landed at Kinghorn, in Fife. A few days later the Scots were routed at the Battle of Dupplin Moor, near Perth. Donald was killed. The poisoned chalice was immediately passed to David's uncle, Andrew Murray, guardian number four. He lasted two months before falling into the hands of Balliol's men and being taken to England where he spent two years as a captive before being allowed to return to Scotland. He at least didn't lose his life, and would eventually resume his guardianship. For the moment, yet another, fifth, guardian had to be found. The privilege fell to Archibald Douglas, cousin of the excommunicated James.

While the Bruce party was seeking to recover from the shambles of Dupplin Moor, Balliol was crowned king at Scone in September 1332, after which it was time to make payment for the tacit support he had received from the English king. At Roxburgh in November 1332, the Scottish king acknowledged he held the throne only by virtue of grant from his feudal overlord, Edward of England. At a stroke, independence, and more, had been surrendered, for Balliol also ceded to Edward large swathes of southern Scotland, including Edinburgh, Roxburgh, Selkirk and Berwick. Another term of the agreement directly affected poor Joan Make Peace. Her marriage to David not having been consummated, she was to be married off to Balliol. And to complete these new arrangements, at a parliament in York the English king rescinded the Treaty of Edinburgh Northampton – ratified by him under duress in 1328 – as a shameful peace.

And so, only three years after Robert's death it appeared as if all he had done had been undone: before his emergence a Plantagenet English king was overlord of Scotland with a subservient Scottish Balliol king as his vassal, and so was the case now – for Edward I and John Balliol read Edward III and Edward Balliol. Was the Bruce dynasty, and Scottish independence, mere illusion? No, far from it. Balliol proved to be as hapless as his father and his band of Disinherited proved no match for those within the Scottish nobility who had gained under Robert's leadership and patronage. In the same month, December 1332, as the English king was announcing his overlordship, Balliol was fleeing Scotland for Carlisle, the victim of a surprise attack led by the guardian Archibald. At last, for the moment, a guardian of the young King David had achieved something other than death or capture.

As one year gave way to the next, the early months of 1333 saw both kingdoms preparing for war. Edward saw no need for diplomacy or delay. He was a warrior king, intent on following in his grandfather's footsteps while simultaneously avenging his father's humiliation. Berwick was to be re-taken. Edward was at Pontefract in March making arrangements. Say hello again to the siege engine. Three were transported from Hull on three ships, the Gracedieu, Jonete, and Nicholas. What types of engine were on board is not documented (so you're spared a second lesson in Greek or Latin) but from the number of boulders heading north, 671 to be precise, it may be reasonably inferred that at least one was a trebuchet. No sign of a walking wardrobe on this occasion, however.

In addition to these traditional weapons of medieval warfare it is more likely than not that a new, revolutionary weapon was added; the firearm. Hence the reason for Edward ordering the manufacture of gunpowder for delivery to the town from a York apothecary. Edward's feudal army was summoned from over the length and breadth of England and Wales: as well as men from the north-east, at the forefront were forces from Yorkshire, Lancashire, Derby and Nottingham. Waiting in the wings were troops from the Welsh marches, Warwick, Leicester and Shropshire. For their part, the Scots took considerable steps to further strengthen the town's timber defensive walls, into which were built nineteen towers, each one equipped with a fighting platform. Under the watchful eye of Sir Alexander Seaton, a Bruce party man through and through, the necessities of life were stockpiled in anticipation of the siege to come. And come it did. It began in mid-March and for weeks the walls were pounded by siege engine missiles while Edward made his way north. Upon arriving outside Berwick on 23rd April, he immediately intensified the pressure by ordering that the water supply to the town be cut off through the destruction of four aqueducts serving it. The English king achieved this preliminary objective with ease, having miners and mercenary setters dig by and sand rake the wooden supports of the aqueducts before setting them alight.

The first full scale attack was by sea, led by one John Crabb, the same Crabb who had been instrumental in securing the town's defences in the 1319 siege. Turncoat. Even, however, with his intimate knowledge of the strengths and weaknesses of the town's defences, the assault was successfully, though simultaneously catastrophically, repulsed when a fire storm, deliberately started by the Scots to keep the English at arm's length, was caught in the gusting North Sea wind and blown back over the walls, setting fire to the timber dwellings along the quayside and spreading into the centre of the town.

This first assault was also the last. Having an overwhelming military advantage, and free of the error-prone ways of his father, Edward could have taken the town at almost any time from late June, by which time suffering and starvation prevailed within the walls. As Ridpath puts it, the town '*was reduced to its last gasp; a rat, a dog, a cat was sold for almost its weight in money; the horses were slaughtered for food.*' No change there, then.

Edward's desire, however, for his first glorious military success was not to be sated merely by the town's surrender. He was a warrior king; only victory in open battle would be sufficient. In an echo of Bannockburn, only with the roles of besieger and besieged reversed, a fifteen day truce was agreed, to end on 11th July. If by that date the town had not been relieved by a Scottish force it would be handed over to Edward. As security, twelve hostages taken from Berwick's leading families were delivered into the English camp. Now the Scots, the guardian Archibald Douglas in particular, faced a dilemma: should battle be joined with the English army or should Berwick – the town for which Robert Bruce and Archibald's cousin, James, were willing to suffer everlasting damnation – be meekly handed back to the Plantagenets? Douglas hesitated. It was not until the final day of the truce that he made his move. In the early hours of 11th July, the Scottish force crossed the Tweed at Yair Ford. With the English encamped some distance away on the hill at Sunnyside, the Scots laid waste to the village of Tweedmouth and were even able to supply the town with much needed relief before the English fleet took control of the river. A second echo, this time of the 1319 siege. In addition to the assault on Tweedmouth, the Scots, in the hope of drawing Edward away, besieged the castle at Bamburgh. The significance of this act lay in the fact that at the castle Edward's queen, Philippa, was in residence.

The Bamburgh ruse was Archibald's equivalent of Robert's surge into Yorkshire. It was, on this occasion, too little too late. Edward knew Berwick would fall before Bamburgh did. Philippa was perfectly safe. And the Scots' assertion that they had rescued the town by managing to get 200 men inside its walls left Edward unpersuaded. He saw the situation in simple terms: the period of truce had expired, the town ought to have been surrendered to him; it hadn't been, and, consequently, the lives of the twelve hostages were forfeit. Without further ado, gallows were built on the south side of the river at Hang-a-Dyke Nook. The first hostage to feel the hangman's noose around his neck was Thomas Seaton, the son of the warden, Alexander, who, with Thomas' mother, watched from the river's north bank as the third of their three sons to lose his life in the cause of Scotland's independence was executed. Their first was killed in 1332 in the Dupplin Moor debacle and their second in the skirmish for control of the river and sea during the guardian's Tweedmouth assault.

On Edward's orders the remaining hostages were to be executed one by one until the town was given up to him. Upon learning of this, the defenders' will buckled, but did not entirely break. Negotiations were re-commenced, with Edward a willing party to them as he remained determined to have his day in the field. A further short truce was agreed. Its principal term was that if the town had not been relieved by the evening of 19th July both the castle and the town would be surrendered at sunrise on 20th. Another, on the face of it surprising, provision was that the newly appointed warden of the town, Sir William Keith (a fine name if ever there was one) and two other noblemen were allowed through the English ranks to seek out the guardian, Archibald Douglas, who was with his forces harrying the communities of north Northumberland in the vain hope of diverting Edward away from the siege, to apprise him of this latest, and final, truce. Surprising, that is, until you remember Edward's principal wish was to do battle with the Scots.

A third echo, Robert's voice. Douglas could hear Robert's deathbed plea; avoid open battle with the English. A dilemma. Should he heed Robert's words and allow the Scottish army, which in all probability outnumbered its English counterpart, perhaps by as much as two to one, to drift away, and thereby surrender Berwick up to Edward, or instead accept the challenge and, if successful, write his name in Scotland's history as a military leader, the equal of the Wallace and Robert?

Tragically, he chose to do battle. Having gathered an army from all parts of Scotland, Douglas perhaps thought he was prepared, but this Edward's army would not be sent homeward to think again. In the early morning of 19th July, Douglas' army set off on a march from Duns. Edward, however, had already crossed to the north side of the Tweed and drawn up his forces at Halidon Hill. Douglas led his army on to higher ground nearby, at Witches Knowe. The attack would begin at midday, when the tide was at its highest, to prevent an English retreat across the river; the foe would drown in the Tweed just as those before them had drowned in the Bannock burn.

But to attack the English position the Scots had to descend the Knowe, trudge through the boggy ground separating it from Halidon Hill and then climb the steep ascent of Heavyside. The climb commenced; then, a pause. From the Scots' ranks out stepped one of their legendary soldiers, Turnbull, a man of goliath like proportions famous for having saved the life of Robert by slaying a wild boar. Turnbull, standing with his mastiff dog within an arrow's shot of the English army, sought single combat with any opponent prepared to face him. From the English mass stepped a young Norfolk knight, Richard of Benhal. The mastiff sprang at Richard's throat only to be cut asunder with a single stroke of the knight's sword.

Turnbull was next, his head cut off and held aloft by Richard as a trophy and encouragement to the English forces. Silence descended, a sense perhaps on both sides that the outcome of the battle to come had already been decided, broken on the English side by the sound of a feudal horn, a trialist from Lincolnshire having the privilege of playing the haunting melody that caused the Scottish host to hesitate. Then came a sudden rush as the Scots, committed as they were to battle, charged up Halidon Hill.

Their amour, however, was no match for what met them from the brow of the hill as a hail of arrows, each 32 inches long, of ash, oak and birch unleashed from the longbows of six divisions of English archers, rained down upon them. It was a rout. By the end, there was barely a Scot left standing. David's guardian number five was dead. Douglas Dyke, a narrow lane leading over the top of the hill, is said to mark the spot where he was slain. With him, to heaven or to hell, went a great swathe of the Scottish nobility, together with the country's decimated army.

Keith Ryan

Lessons in Scottish warfare no.1

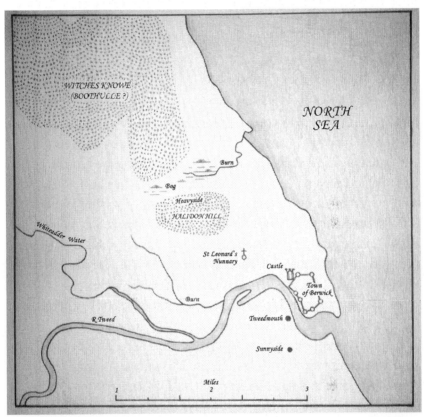

Do not march fifteen miles, charge down one hill, trudge through a bog and then charge up another hill into a hail of arrows and expect to win the day. Descending from Witches Knowe and then crossing boggy land before commencing the climb up Heavyside, the Scottish army was surely exhausted even before it was brought to its knees by the hail storm of English and Welsh arrows that greeted its arrival.

Thomas of Eyemouth was a twentieth century soothsayer and descendant of Thomas of Earlston. On 14th June 1996 he was in Dunbar, entertaining the Tartan Army before it headed off for its Euro '96 sporting assault on England's capital city the following day. What he had to say, however, was hardly entertaining:

85

*'Woe worth the morrow, for it will be a day of disaster
and woe, a very great and bitter day in the kingdom; after
noon such a wind shall blow as has never been heard of
for many years, and the blast of it shall humble lofty hearts
and level the high places of the hills.'*

At Wembley the following afternoon, I was sitting with my head in my hands, heartbroken, ruing Gary McAllister's penalty miss and wondering how it could have happened. How could he miss from twelve yards? As I lifted my head I saw Colin Hendry sprawled on the ground as Paul Gascoigne volleyed into the Scottish net. Just like their July 1333 ancestors, the Scots knew the game was up. It was my very own, personal, Halidon Hill, although I suppose some comfort was had in the fact that, after Wembley at least, the vanquished lived to see another day. Some years afterwards I realised Thomas had been right; the answer to the McAllister question, my friend, was blowin' in the wind.

History would unfold otherwise, but in the immediate aftermath of the battle it seemed that Scotland would finally become a mere fiefdom of England, and in becoming Scotland's overlord, Edward would succeed where his father and grandfather had failed. As for Berwick, it opened its gates and gave up its castle to Edward. The pendulum had swung; for the time being the town was once again English.

As an offering of thanks to his maker, Edward donated the sum of £20 per annum towards the repair of St Leonard's Convent and Church situated at the foot of the battlefield, whose Cistercian nuns had tended the wounded on both sides. The English troops celebrated their victory in the Heavy Battery; if you're not sure where that is, just call into the Brewers Arms in Marygate and ask for directions.

In defeating the Scots in open battle and immediately upon doing so taking possession of the town, Edward had in an instant avenged the humiliations heaped on his father at Bannockburn and the 1319 siege. It must also have seemed at the time that in becoming Scotland's overlord, acting through his vassal king, Edward Balliol, the English king would finally subdue the Scottish nation and in so doing better the feats of his grandfather. The true hammer of the Scots would be Edward the warrior king, not his grandfather. But history unfolded otherwise. Edward did not linger long in Berwick. By early August 1333 he had returned south, leaving Balliol, with the assistance of English military support, to establish himself in Scotland. At first, he did so with relative ease. The near obliteration of the Bruce party at Halidon Hill enabled Balliol to return to Scotland unopposed and, in his first post-return parliament he at a stroke sought to undo all that had gone before in the short-lived Bruce dynasty by revoking all grants of land and titles made to the Bruce party and returning them to the previously dispossessed, the Disinherited.

There was little, indeed nothing, the rump Bruce party could do at that stage to oppose the Balliol/Plantagenet ascendancy. Were it not for the limited support of Philip VI of France, who provided safe haven in the form of a Normandy chateau for the ten year old David, his queen, and a modest court in May 1334, Robert's dynasty would in all probability have been extinguished. Just a month later, the deal agreed by Balliol and Edward was completed when the Scottish king completed the handover to his English overlord of the town and county of Berwick, Roxburgh, Edinburgh, Haddington, Linlithgow, Peebles, Dumfries, the Forest of Selkirk, Jedburgh and Hawick. Southern Scotland had become northern England.

But Balliol's reign never took hold. Having handed over half of Scotland to Edward he could not, partly for that very reason, find acceptance in the other half as the vassal, puppet king of his English opposite number.

Before we leave Halidon Hill you might want to have a look at the battle site, which is within reasonable walking distance of the town centre. You'll need a couple of spare hours and a decent pair of walking shoes or boots; I'm particularly fond of Spanish boots of Spanish leather. If you want a map for comfort I suggest taking no. 346 of the Ordnance Survey's 'Explorer Series'.

To Halidon Hill and back

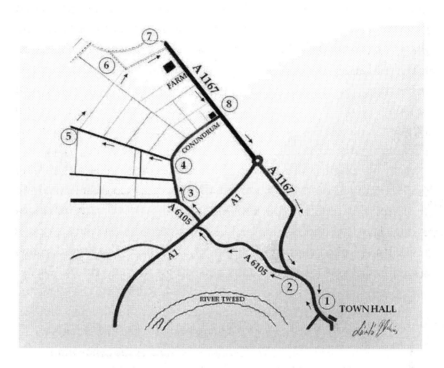

From the Town Hall (1), walk straight up the street (Marygate) through the Scotsgate arch, into Castlegate. Continue up past the Free Trade on your left, avoiding, if you are able, the temptation to call in for a pint, until you reach the top of Castlegate, where in front of you is the road bridge over the main east coast train line. Cross the bridge and, once over, take a left turn on to the A6105 signposted for the A1 South and Kelso (2). You now need to mind your 'Ps & Qs' for you are entering Castle Terrace, where the well-to-do live. In my early teens I had a Saturday job at the local butcher's shop, R. Norris. On my old fashioned basket bicycle I delivered meat to Castle Terrace and to Prior Park, the council housing estate where I grew up. Better tips in Prior Park.

At the end of Castle Terrace the road bends to the right and becomes

Duns Road. Ahead of you is the Berwick A1 bypass. Cross the A1 and continue along the A1605. Unlike the Plantagenets, I have no wish to have blood on my hands, so be careful crossing. About half a mile on, turn into the lane on your right (3); it goes up and over the eastern side of the hill. Ignore the first footpath sign you reach; it is on a circular walk you are not following. Instead, carrying on up the hill you arrive at a viewpoint and information board. It is worthwhile stopping here for a few minutes; there are glorious views of the Tweed Valley and the Cheviots. If you have a look at the picture on the information board you'll see, on the south side of the river, two corpses hanging from a tree – Hang-a-Dyke Nook.

On leaving the viewpoint and continuing uphill, take a left turn into the lane immediately past the triangulation mast (4). In due course you will see on your right the battle site marker (5) (it would be something of an exaggeration to refer to it as a monument). It bears the words of one of the protagonists, regrettably unnamed, on the English side. His words are noteworthy for their lack of triumphalism, and their hint of pathos:

'From the top of Halidon Hill we could clearly see the Scots approaching. Their army was much larger than ours but only by swinging to the north behind a hill that was higher than Halidon could they take us by surprise. The king deployed us on the north facing slope of the hill. We were formed into three divisions, each division being flanked by archers. It was an ideal defensive site with trees at the summit and boggy land at the base. The earl of Norfolk commanded the right, the king led the centre, and Edward Balliol took the left. ... The Scots then advanced towards us. As they stumbled around in the boggy ground our archers cut them down with volley after volley of arrows. Those that made it out of the bog started to climb the slope towards us and were cut down by our knights. The smell of blood and the cries of dying men, carried to us by the wind on that blustery day, was appalling.'

To begin your return to town, walk down past the marker, the boundary of the field right having a line of relatively newly planted trees. At the foot of the hill (6) keep the field boundary, now a barbed wire fence, on your right. This is the only part of the walk where, if you have no sense of direction, you could possibly go awry. Do not take the path on the right side of the fence. Assuming you're still on the correct path, after a few hundred yards you will reach a gate-less opening in the fence. Go through the opening; turn immediately to your left and then a few yards on sharply to your right. If at this point you can't see the sea ahead in the distance you've gone the wrong way. With a barbed wire fence on your right, walk downhill to a wooden gate. Going through the gate, take a sharp turn right and then more or less immediately turn left on to a well-defined track going downhill towards the A1. At the foot of the hill the track bends to the right (7), running parallel to the road. At the end of the track is Loughend Farm, at the front of which there is a tarmac lane, again running parallel to the road. At the end of the lane there is another farmhouse, at Conundrum (8), which is where you will once again meet the A1. A right turn will take you back into the town centre. You'll need to cross the A1 once more, this time just before the bypass roundabout.

Chapter Nine
We Three Kings

Despite being few in number, the Bruce stalwarts who remained in Scotland after the trauma of Halidon Hill – another Douglas (this one was William, cousin of James and Archibald), another Andrew Murray and Robert Stewart (otherwise known as Robert the Steward, the seventeen year old nephew of King David) – led a guerrilla war type resistance against the new regime to such a successful extent that, harried and harassed, Balliol was back in the safe refuge of Berwick by early 1335. The simple truth of the matter was that he was completely dependent on Edward and English military support. Without it, his reign was untenable. During those times when Edward campaigned in Scotland, which he did intermittently in the several years from 1334, Balliol was secure, but when his English ally wasn't on hand he preferred to stay on the south side of the border. On one occasion he didn't even feel safe within the walls of Berwick, sojourning instead on Holy Island.

Ultimately, Edward proved to be a fickle friend. He had avenged his father and at least matched his grandfather; but why settle for being overlord of Scotland, a nation that stubbornly refused to bow, when he had claim to a much grander prize, king of France? Edward's mother, the treacherous Isabella, oh Isabella, proud Isabella, wife of Edward II and female part in the dastardly duo that was Mortimer and Isabella, happened also to be the daughter of King Philip IV of France, who had died in 1314. I am guessing you do not want a thousand words on the genealogy of the French royal family, in particular the Capetian and

Valois branches, so just trust me on this; Edward had a good, meritorious claim to the French throne, at least as legitimate as the incumbent, Philip VI.

Never shy in stating his case or hampered by modesty, Edward in 1337 started referring to himself as king of France and promptly went to war with the French to prove it. One hundred and sixteen years later, it ended. The Hundred Years War had gone into extra time and penalties. England lost. The Match of the Day edited highlights showed that England were winning deep into the second half, with notable contributions from Edward and Henry V. It was Henry's team mates who, after Agincourt, first used the gesture still loved by football fans – the 'V' sign – to their French opponents. The story goes, and really it doesn't matter whether it's true or not, that the French forces threatened that after the battle they would cut off the middle, bow fingers of the English archers. When the French lost, their opponents delighted in showing them their fingers remained intact.

It was a substitution that caused the problem. When the fifth Henry was replaced by his son, the sixth Henry, the match turned, not least because of bickering in the English camp over who should captain the team, the Lancashire Henry or his Yorkshire cousin (sorry about this, it's yet another Edward), Edward IV. In time, the dispute between them would come to be known as the Wars of the Roses and, as you'll see if you carry on reading, it was a war that provided a defining scene in the story of Bloody Berwick.

Back for the moment to our current Edward. While he was away campaigning on the continent, his puppet king was failing miserably. A peace plan offered to David by Balliol in 1336 had been rejected, hardly surprisingly, as in return for a promise he would be king again on Balliol's death David was invited to give up not only his crown but also his wife and queen, Joan, to Balliol. "Won't you come see me, Queen Joan," was the message the man who was determined to replace her husband sent to the Scottish queen.

Without significant English forces to assist him, Balliol was iso-lated. By 1340 most of Scotland was in the possession of the reinvig-orated Bruce party, with the admittedly significant exceptions of the castles of Stirling, Edinburgh, Roxburgh and Berwick. By the spring of 1341, however, one of the four – Edinburgh – had been re-taken. Edward didn't, at this time at any rate, abandon Balliol entirely. When not in France the English king was for the most part in and around the Scottish borders, and Easter 1341 saw him at Berwick castle organis-ing and enjoying a chivalric diversion in the form of a jousting match. In the castle yard twelve Scottish knights took up lances against an equal number of English knights. The English were victorious by two fatalities to one.

With Balliol becoming an increasingly marginalised figure, and Edward unable or unwilling to deploy sufficient military resources in Scotland to curtail the Bruce party resurgence, and Robert Stewart (aka 'the Steward') acting more like king than heir, it was time for the seventeen year old David to establish his personal rule in Scotland. The game of aristocratic musical chairs that was the guardianship of the realm was about to come to an end. Given that four guardians out of five had perished in the role, perhaps Scotland's nobility breathed a collective sigh of relief when on 2nd June 1341 David arrived with his queen, Joan, and senior members of the Bruce party at Inverbevie on the north-east coast of Scotland between Montrose and Stonehaven. His protective exile in France had ended.

It was a time of continuing Scottish success. Roxburgh fell in March 1342, and Stirling a month later, leaving only Berwick on David's agenda. There was to be no direct assault on the town, however. David preferred the tried and tested, and, in terms of ensuring hollow, mean-ingless military success and plunder for his forces, significantly simpler approach of incursions into northern England. Newcastle proved resil-ient, Durham less so. For David, that was far enough for the time being, especially with news arriving that Edward, his campaigning in France temporarily put on hold, was on the march. In the north Northumbrian countryside, Wark castle came into the view of the homeward-bound Scots force. The temptation to add to the plunder already in hand proving irresistible, a siege duly commenced. However, half asleep from celebrating their less than glorious wasting of the county, the Scots failed to notice the governor of the fortress slipping through their midst to apprise Edward of their whereabouts and warn him of the danger posed to the castle. On receiving the news, Edward made haste with his army to Wark to give battle. He was denied the opportunity for further military glory when David, wisely, withdrew his forces and headed back over the border. Edward's Wark expedition was not, however, without its compensations as he was greeted warmly (Ridpath hints a little too warmly) by the castle's principal resident, the alluring countess of Salisbury, whose husband happened to be elsewhere. It was in honour of the countess that Edward subsequently founded that most noble chivalrous body, the Order of the Garter. And, God forbid, for any of you who think there may have been some impropriety in their relationship, all I can say is *honi soit qui mal y pense.*

By having his army return to Scotland rather than confront the English in battle in the Northumbrian countryside, David had followed his late father's deathbed plea. For the three or so years following the Wark episode the young Scottish king concentrated his efforts, with considerable success, on consolidating his position and ensuring his seven-year protective exile in France had not caused any long lasting damage to his kingship. His heir (David being childless) and rival, Robert Steward, remained on the scene but not in a position of sufficient strength to pose a real danger to David's personal rule. And, for one of the very few times in the long, interrupted, unsatisfactory history of the auld alliance, Scotland was an equal – it would be stretching it too far to say the dominant – partner to France. By letter of 20th June 1346, Philip's entreaty to David was this:

'I beg you, I implore you with all the force I can, to remember the bonds of blood and friendship between us. Do for me what I would willingly do for you in such a crisis, and do it quickly and thoroughly as with God's help you are able.'

Crisis, what crisis? What possible crisis could be facing the French king that he would have cause to write in such imploring terms to his poor relation? The answer took the form of Edward Plantagenet, otherwise known as Edward King of France, who was knocking on Philip's door. Only a month after his first correspondence, Philip put pen to paper again, describing his desperate plight to David and, none too subtly, hinting at how the Scottish king could help – *'The English king has... most of his army with him here, another division in Gascony and yet another in Flanders... [meanwhile all of England] is a defenceless void.'*

Attack, attack, attack, was the message. Invade northern England. Create a diversion of enough magnitude to force Edward to divide his forces and fight on two fronts. David was slow, very slow, to react. Even after the first significant land battle of the war on French soil, at Crecy in August 1346 when the French army was all but annihilated, he kept his forces safely ensconced north of the border. The summer came and went. Eventually, in October, too late to assist Philip, but with plunder, tribute money and glory, in that order, foremost in mind the Scottish army crossed the border in the south-west, wasted several villages and other small settlements, studiously avoiding the more demanding target of Carlisle, before turning eastwards into Northumberland but not, however, to threaten either Newcastle or Berwick. Instead, the Scots changed direction again and advanced southwards towards Durham, their march bearing a greater resemblance to an ostentatious, complacent royal progression than a vengeful invasion. Pomp and circumstance. The young King David was in his element. With Edward campaigning in France, plunder was assured and the glory of success in battle was about to be served up to him on a platter by the smallest of English armies, mustered by the stay-at-home northern barons of England and the forgotten, nearly king of Scotland, Balliol.

When I say that nothing stood in David's way you know, rightly, that it will be followed by a but; in fact, two buts. The first but was complacency. Remember, Robert shouted in his son's ear, what I said on my deathbed, remember also your good sense in declining open battle at Wark. David ignored him. The second but was treachery or cowardice, or possibly both. Look up the Battle of Neville's Cross; the battle site is slightly west of Durham. It is not one much remembered – England doesn't need to because there were so many other successful encounters against the Scots, and Scotland doesn't want to because it is just another in a long line of defeats inflicted upon it by its southern neighbour – better just to remember Stirling Bridge and Bannockburn, and the Wembley Wizards of 1967.

Going one better than Harold at the Battle of Hastings, David played host to two arrows in his face. As he lay stricken, defended by a handful of his most loyal lieutenants, his nephew and next in line to the throne, the Steward, withdrew. The king is dead, long live the king was no doubt the thought uppermost in the Steward's mind as he raced northwards towards the border. Except the king wasn't dead. Miraculously, David survived. The monk surgeons of the day removed one arrow barb from his face, leaving the other as a permanent, painful reminder of his hubris as, captive, he was transported from the battlefield to Wark castle and then on to the fortress of Bamburgh before finally taking up residence at the English king's pleasure in the Tower of London.

Fast forward. Not too far. Fewer than ten years. It is 1355. David remains incarcerated in reasonable if not royal comfort in England, still two years away from a return to his native land; Edward continues to cause havoc in France; and a low level war of attrition is the order of the day in Scotland, with Scots raiding parties nipping to no great effect at the heels of the English garrison in Berwick. The Scottish king had sought to engineer his release on terms that in the event he died without an heir the Scottish throne would pass to the English Plantagenets. He was disabused of any hope that his compatriots would find the proposal acceptable at a Scone parliament in February 1352. The warning to Robert in the Declaration of Arbroath - *'Yet Robert himself, should he turn aside from the task that he has begun, and yield Scotland or us to the English King and people, we should cast out as the enemy of us all, as subverter of our rights and of his own, and should choose another king to defend our freedom'* – could not have been far from the parliament's thoughts when it rejected the proposed deal with a stinging rebuke to David; if his freedom was to be secured it would not be at the expense of his country's sovereignty.

By 1355 the French stage had witnessed the exit of Philip VI and the succession of his son, John II. Prepare yourself for another climb up the scaling ladders. King John, or John the Good as his countrymen affectionately remember him, exhibiting a distinct lack of originality of thought, came up with a plan that, to divert Edward from his French campaign, the auld alliance should be invoked to persuade the Scots to attack northern England. In June of that year 60 men at arms, under the command of a French knight – Eugene de Garantiere – arrived in Scotland with 40,000 crowns for distribution between those Scots whom it was thought were worth bribing to take part in the campaign. Once the inevitable squabbling over how the windfall was to be divided had been resolved, though not to the satisfaction of everyone, the usual pattern of raids into north Northumberland recommenced. And on this occasion Berwick, too, was targeted.

From a fleet of ships, funded from what remained of the Good King John's 40,000 crowns, under cover of darkness on a bitterly cold, wind and rain swept, blood-freezing November night only the North Sea can conjure up, a combined Scottish and French force disembarked at

Magdalen Fields. Too late to visit the Pilot, the main body set up an unfired camp for the night and did what it could to endure the wind and rain while the magnates passed a much warmer and infinitely more comfortable time in the company of an obliging hostess; come in, she said, I'll give you shelter from the storm. The attack commenced at dawn. The guard at Cowport had mysteriously vanished, allowing the Scots to scale the wall and open the gate unopposed.

Taken completely by surprise, the town's garrison was easily over-powered; the captain of the town, Sir Alexander Ogle, and two other knights were killed. The townsfolk fled, many into the castle through the Douglas Tower, leaving their possessions behind. In plunder terms, it was yet another successful enterprise for the Scots. A little bit of Latin for you – *aura & argente et divitiis infiustis* – gold and silver and infinite wealth is what I'm reliably told it means. But, so far as securing the town permanently was concerned, better than silver and gold for the Scots would have been the capture of the castle. They failed; the taking of the Douglas Tower – an antechamber of the castle – was to be the limit of their achievement.

Symbolically, it was Robert Steward who entered the town to mark its return to Scottish jurisdiction, king in all but name while David languished in England. If, in the shortest of runs, the campaign had been a resounding success for the Scots, the same could also be said, however again only in the short term, for their auld alliance partner, John the Good. His plan had worked, but on this occasion the pendulum's swing was very short. As soon as Edward, who was at the time pursuing his grand campaign in France, received news of the fall of the town he returned immediately to Westminster from where a summons was issued for an army, predominantly of Welsh and northern English bowmen, to muster at Newcastle. After spending only three days in London, Edward headed for Berwick. By 14th January 1256 he and his army had reached the town and his fleet sat in wait at the river's mouth. Having entered the castle from the river, the king's first act in making arrangements for the pending attack was to have miners, brought especially from the Forest of Dean, apply their expertise by laying explosive charges at strategic points against the base of the walls. The fourth English siege in 60 years had begun. It was over very quickly. Barely a day later the Scottish garrison, realising assistance in the form of a relieving army would not be forthcoming, agreed, in return for its freedom, to surrender the town without any show of resistance. No bare backsides, fire fights, or wrecking of siege engines this time around; just an inglorious but eminently sensible capitulation.

What this episode demonstrated was the continuing importance of the town to the English king. Whereas a decade earlier he had been content to remain in France and leave the northern English magnates to respond to the Scots' invasion, the moment in late 1355 he was apprised of the loss of Berwick he abandoned, albeit temporarily, his French campaign in favour of personally leading the expedition to re-take the town. Achieving his objective, however, was not sufficient to satisfy his desire for retribution against the Scots who, he could hardly believe, had been willing to act so aggressively while their own king remained captive in England. The Plantagenet's blood was up. What followed the re-taking of Berwick was one of the bloodiest, most horrific, episodes of the wars of independence, in which Edward matched and surpassed even the most heinous deeds of his father and grandfather.

The second day of February is Candlemas, a Christian festival of celebration. It marks the 40th day after the birth of Jesus, when Mary presented him to God at the temple in Jerusalem. It is also the midpoint between winter solstice and spring equinox, a time for looking forward, for optimism, with spring light approaching with every passing day. There was to be no such optimism, no festival of the coming light, for the people of Lothian in Scotland. From Berwick the English army marched rapidly to Roxburgh, where the destruction of people and property commenced. In Lothian, the barbarians advanced through a twenty-mile-wide corridor, indulging in an orgy of destruction and murder as they went along. Edinburgh and Haddington, where even the resident Franciscan monks weren't spared from the flames, were the worst affected. With those who could fleeing north of the Forth to avoid Edward's wrath, this was the English king's revenge; Burnt Candlemas, for the Scots daring to interrupt his campaign across the Channel.

February 1356 was notable for one other event of passing significance, the final exiting from the stage of the third king in the war of the three kings; Balliol. For once, death was not the cause of the adieu. No, in Balliol's case, age and embitterment were the twin persuasive factors. In his seventies and heirless, Balliol finally gave up the ghost. At Roxburgh castle he presented to the English king a handful of Scottish soil – Scotland in microcosm – in return for an annuity of £2,000 and, echoing his father's bilious view of the Scottish people, gave up his claim to kingship over them with these words:

> *'I wholly, simply, and absolutely yield unto thee my cause,*
> *and all right I have, or may have, to the throne of Scotland,*
> *so that thou avenge me of my enemies, the Scottish nation,*
> *a race most false, who have always cast me aside, that I*
> *should not reign over them.'*

By this time, however, Balliol's fickle Plantagenet ally was also losing interest, for in truth although Edward took undoubted satisfaction in venting his fury on the Scottish nation – amply demonstrated by Burnt Candlemas – his wish to rule the country, either directly or indirectly through a feudal vassal king, had waned considerably.

It wasn't long before Edward was back in France, where he was soon to enjoy yet more military glory, one consequence of which was that David, still captive in England, had the pleasure of some royal company. September 1356 saw one of Edward's greatest moments, delivered to him courtesy of the military prowess of his son the Black

Prince (we'll not refer to him by his first name because we've already had more than our fair share of Edwards and there are more to come) and the advice given to the French generals by their hapless Scottish advisors, who thought a reprise of the Bannockburn battle plan would win the day for the auld alliance. They were sorely mistaken. At Poitiers, the English and Welsh archers, repeating the strategy that had served so well at Halidon Hill and Crecy, took credit for giving the prince's army an initial advantage and creating the momentum for the ensuing rout. Within a couple of hours, the auld alliance was no more and the French king, John the Good, acquired the new title of John the Captive as the English pastime of king-collecting continued.

Having company turned out to be good news for David. True, he fell down the pecking order of VIPs (very important prisoners), a king of France trumping a king of Scotland by a very considerable margin, but it also meant Edward was more willing than had hitherto been the case to contemplate permitting his brother-in-law to return to his native land. And no longer interested in acquiring the Scottish crown – the realisation of his aspiration to be crowned king of France was beckoning – all that had to be negotiated was the ransom. Negotiations between magnate representatives of the two countries opened in Berwick in August 1357. Progress was swift, sufficiently so that David was in September permitted, notionally under guard, to travel north to the town, accompanied by a small entourage. On 3rd October the Treaty of Berwick was signed and three days later David, a free man, headed homeward tae rule again.

The terms of the treaty were financially extremely onerous. Scotland was to pay to the English crown the sum of 100,000 marks in equal instalments over ten years, the money to be handed over at Berwick provided the town remained under English control and if not at either Norham or Bamburgh. The instalments were to be paid each year on 24th June, Midsummer's Day, the anniversary of Bannockburn. Clearly, someone on the English side had a sense of humour.

There was never any realistic prospect of the Scottish exchequer finding the monies to pay the ransom. The first instalment was made on time; the second was late; the third is still in the post. Well, no that's not quite true. David spent the best part of a decade seeking to renegotiate the terms of the treaty, eventually persuading Edward to accept a sum of 56,000 marks spread over fourteen years from 1370, the date for payment varied to Candlemas each year. The initial instalment of 4,000 marks was duly made at Candlemas 1370 in Berwick. By the time the second was due David had made his final exit. Six years later, in June 1377, he was followed by his English brother-in-law and soul mate in chivalry, Edward, who, by the end, had metamorphosed from handsome, young warrior king into obese, lecherous loser. Crecy and Poitiers were irrelevant, distant memories of his failed imperial aspirations. All gone, save for a port town in north-western France. Hail! Edward, King of Calais. Not, in truth, much of an epitaph.

So, who are the new actors on the stage? Let's introduce them in chronological order of appearance.

David died without issue. He was succeeded by his nephew, Robert Stewart, who thus became, as Robert II, the first of the Stewart monarchs. As for England, we mercifully get some respite from the dreaded E word; our new man on the block (that is almost a pun but not quite) is Richard II.

During the relatively short reigns of the mark twos Robert and Richard, Berwick town remained untroubled, fortified to the hilt to keep the Scots at bay. Surprisingly, however, the castle proved vulnerable. On the feast of St Andrew 1378, the castle garrison somehow managed to find itself defeated in an attack by seven fine men from the Scottish borders. They killed the castle governor but were chivalrous enough to allow his wife and children to go free on condition that a ransom was paid within three weeks. In the event of default, mother and children were to return to their castle captivity. Given their antecedents, the gallant rebels' purported allegiance was, to say the least, a little off the wall. On receiving the inevitable ultimatum to hand the castle back or face the fatal consequences of declining to do so, in unison they replied defiantly, *'We shall neither yield it to the King of England, nor the King of Scotland, but will defend it against all mortals for the King of France.'* Les Sept Magnifiques. And more. Forty-eight, *quarante-huit*, in the end, held out for a full eight days against (this is surely an exaggeration) 7,000 English archers and 3,000 horsemen. On the ninth day, defending the castle to the last, 47 of the 48 magnificents met their end. One was spared for a brief time for the purposes of interrogation. The English wished to know whether the assault on the castle was the precursor of a reinvigorated auld alliance invasion. Robert II was equally curious.

The castle fell to the Scots for a second time in Richard's reign, in 1384 after the end of a fourteen-year truce, the Great Truce, which had been entered into at Berwick in November 1360 by John of Gaunt (lieutenant of the eastern march) and commissioners for the Scottish king. There was little of the magnificent or heroic in this episode; the Scots took it upon paying a bribe (sum unknown) to the castle's Deputy Governor, and subsequently relinquished it to the Earl of Northumberland in consideration of payment of 2,000 marks, presumably making a handsome profit from the transaction.

Not much else to say, really, about the town in the reigns of Robert II and Richard II. Robert exited in 1390. Richard, kicking and screaming until his strength deserted him as he starved to death in Pontefract castle, left the scene in 1399.

With the Stewart dynasty now established, a relatively orderly succession saw Robert's eldest son, John, assume the mantle. John the Second. Except he wasn't. He didn't, it seems, like the name. Too much of a risk, he reasoned, of being thought of as a descendant of the universally denigrated John Balliol. For the Scots you can't go wrong with a Robert, and so it was that not King John the Second became Robert the Third (mercifully, at least, sparing us another Edward).

There was nothing orderly about the succession in England. It wasn't even a succession; it was a *coup d'etat* led by Richard's cousin, Henry Bolingbroke. Banished for life in 1398 from this sceptr'd isle by Richard, Henry returned uninvited the following year. With a modest force, he came ashore at Ravenspur, Yorkshire, while the king was off on a hopeless jaunt in Ireland. Henry's ostensible intention was to recover his lands. When, however, on his return Richard imploded in an extended bout of fatalistic pessimism, Bolingbroke widened his horizons to include the throne, which he duly acquired upon Richard's forced abdication. Already having an eminently suitable regal name, Henry was quite content to be the fourth.

As we've seen, the Scots were never slow to have a little foray over the border in search of rich pickings when the opportunity presented itself. Henry's coup gave them just such an opportunity. Wark castle was targeted, relieved of what it housed by way of valuable contents and then reduced. But, sure enough, the new English king, riding high on the back of a swift, ruthless power grab, was not willing to allow this rebellious act to go unpunished. No, like those in whose footsteps he trod, he was determined to bring the Scots to heel. All very interesting and, by now, I'm sure you'll be thinking, perfectly predictable. He'll raise an army, head north and defeat the enemy in battle or, if it refuses to show itself, devastate its lands. Well, yes and no. Certainly, Henry raised an army, 15,000 to 20,000 strong, which crossed into Scotland on 14th August 1400. There the similarity with his forefathers ends, for Henry had fixed upon a uniquely novel means by which to finally and permanently subdue, subjugate and put the fear of God and more into this uncooperative Scottish nation. He sent a letter. You, Robert III, he said, will meet me at Edinburgh castle on 23rd August, where you will bend your knee in homage and acknowledge me as your king and overlord of Scotland, by whose grant you are permitted to be king. When Henry and his troops arrived outside the city's castle on the appointed day, Robert was out, in Bute. Perhaps he hadn't received the letter;

maybe it was lost in the post. Ah, well, never mind, Henry thought, as he marched his army south, perhaps my next letter will be received, though for Henry there never was a next letter or a next time. The moral of the story? If you're going to assert your feudal authority over your vassal, don't do it by post. The most galling aspect of the whole affair was that the Bard wrote not one but two plays about the man.

Chapter Ten
The Devil Comes a' Calling

A little more time travel brings us to a new point on our stage. New players have replaced those who have departed, and the town is calm and settled, having experienced a significant period of respite from war while under English control in the first half of the fifteenth century.

In Scotland, our final Robert has been followed off our stage by the first two of our seven Jameses. Both suffered untimely ends. The first was assassinated by his fellow countrymen in February 1437. The second was a young man, a mere 29 years, when in early August 1460 he and his army settled in on the north side of the Tweed at the commencement of a three-stage action to re-take Roxburgh, then Wark, and finally Berwick. It wasn't the most subtle of plans; it was intended that heavy artillery would be used to bombard each castle's garrison into submission. Amongst the weaponry assembled as the siege of Roxburgh began was the famous Mons Meg, a giant cannon gifted to James in 1457 by Philip the Good, Duke of Burgundy. If you want to have a look at it just pay a visit to Edinburgh castle, where it is on display for all to see.

James number two was very fond, tragically too fond, of this type of heavy artillery. At Roxburgh on 3rd August 1460, standing next to another of his favourite pieces, the Lion, it exploded in his face, killing him on the spot. Notwithstanding the enormity of this setback, the Scots went on over the following several days to conclude the siege successfully and move on to achieve an identical outcome at Wark. Berwick, however, remained in English hands.

Our third James was crowned at Kelso a week after his father's death. Even as a boy of eight, he was aware of the significance of Berwick and his affection for the town matched that of the long since dead Alexander. As we'll see shortly, he took enormous pride in having the town gifted to him by a grateful, if mad, English king, only later as he languished, helpless, a prisoner of his own people, in Edinburgh castle, to suffer the trauma of losing it to Shakespeare's favourite villain.

As for England, the glory days of Crecy, Agincourt and the all-conquering Henry V had, by 1460, given way to defeat to France in the Hundred (and sixteen) Years War and civil war at home between the houses of York and Lancaster, the latter war fought initially for control of the monarch, namely the simple-minded, now insane, Henry VI, and ultimately for the crown itself.

A few paragraphs are required on that confusing, perplexing series of bloody fifteenth century encounters which much, much later came to be known as the Wars of the Roses. This will help us to understand how it came to pass that, in April 1461, Berwick and its castle were presented back to Scotland, and then how, 21 years later, the pendulum swung again, some say (but not me) for the final time.

When in 1422 the still young fifth Henry died at Vincennes, near Paris, while doing what he did best – making the lives of the French a misery – he was succeeded by his son of eight months, our sixth Henry. During the new king's minority, the country was governed by a coterie of councillors appointed to act in his name. So successful were they that by the time Henry's personal rule commenced in 1436 he was the crowned king not only of England but also of France. Over the next twenty years, however, Henry, largely owing to his injudicious military appointments, had engineered England's ignominious defeat to France in the Hundred Years War.

Having lost France save for Calais, Henry in short order also lost his sanity, causing in turn the two most powerful dynasties in the land – the House of Lancaster and the House of York – to take up arms against each other. In the Lancastrian corner were Henry's wife and queen, Margaret of Anjou, and her councillors; in the Yorkist corner was Richard, Duke of York, the king's cousin. In August 1453 Henry, for reasons unknown then and now, lapsed into a state of complete mental incapacity, accompanied by severe physical disability. The struggle for control of the king in these unique circumstances was initially a game of political chess only.

Margaret proposed an arrangement entirely new to England, whereby her husband's powers as king would be transferred to her as regent. York's alternative was more conservative, that he be appointed as Henry's protector with powers identical to those conferred on the council which had ruled in the king's name during his minority. The parties' search for allies within the nobility intensified in October on the birth to Margaret and Henry of a son and heir, Edward (groan). It made York, whose barely hidden agenda was to be crowned king in the event of Henry's failure to recover or, preferably, of his death from his mysterious malady, ever more determined to control events. Finally, the innovative idea of a regency having been rejected, in March 1454 the French queen was checked; York was appointed as the country's protector and defender for so long as Henry remained incapacitated.

Checkmate, however, it was not. Over the six years that followed, Henry recovered his sanity (or so it was claimed), the duke rebelled, claimed the throne for himself, and, ultimately, lost his life in December 1460, at the Battle of Wakefield. The Lancastrians followed up this success with another at St Albans in February 1461.

Checkmate, then, for Henry and his queen? No, on the contrary; the duke's son, whose name it will come as no surprise to you was, yes, Edward, claimed the throne as Edward IV, thereby setting the scene for another bloody aristocratic showdown. The date was Sunday 29th March 1461; the battle site was Towton, a village a few miles south-west of York. Ironically, you may think, the city of York was a Lancastrian stronghold, and settled on the day of the battle within the relative safety of its castle walls were Henry, Margaret his queen, and their thousand-strong entourage. The nineteen year old Edward of York, meanwhile, was at the head of his troops. And so, at eleven o'clock on Palm Sunday morning, in blinding snow, the bloodiest battle ever fought on English soil commenced. Twelve hours later, with snow still falling, the Lancastrian army fell back, defeated. At least 20,000 men had lost their lives in the carnage. News travelled fast. Before midnight, and before what was left of the successful Yorkist army could reach the city, the royal Lancastrian couple, with their entourage and what valuables they could carry, fled north to Berwick and then into Scotland.

Not wishing to miss an opportunity, the council of Scottish noblemen and clergy who governed in the name of the boy King James extended a warm, hospitable welcome to the royal couple, who naturally wished to show their gratitude and appreciation for the sanctuary afforded to them. And this they did by, on 25th April 1861, handing over to Scotland both Berwick town and its castle. That they would have been returned forthwith to their Yorkist enemies if they hadn't done so was surely never put to them.

For the Yorkists, Henry's act in gifting, if that is what it was, the town away was an act of treason, one consequence of which was that Northumberland for years thereafter experienced a continuation of the Wars of the Roses, with Edward directing military resources northward while Henry and those lords still loyal to him, of which there were still a significant number, proving from their base in Scotland the fight had not gone out of them, evidenced by the fact that cross-border raids into Northumberland gave them possession, if only temporarily, of Bamburgh, Dunstanburgh and Alnwick castles.

Sadly for Henry, Scotland proved to be a less than reliable host. On 9th December 1463 (only 526 years to the day before I was married and before the draw for the 1990 World Cup finals – Scotland drawing, *inter alia*, Costa Rica and therefore being certain to progress to the second phase of the competition), recognising that the Yorkist ascendancy was likely to be permanent and therefore in giving succour to Henry it was backing the wrong horse, James' council concluded a peace treaty with Edward's England. Henry was no longer a guest or welcome, and by Christmas he found himself in Bamburgh castle, evicted from his Scottish refuge and a fugitive in his own country. When, shortly afterwards, the castle was no longer a safe haven, he was reduced to becoming an itinerant wanderer in northern England until his capture in Lancashire in 1465. But that wasn't the end of Henry's story, or of the civil war that was the Wars of the Roses. In one of the more bizarre episodes in the history of the English monarchy, he was king again for a brief period from October 1470 until the spring of 1471 when, at last, the civil war was decided once and for all in favour of Edward and his Yorkists.

In Scotland, James in his personal rule after reaching adulthood was a less than popular figure. A penchant for debasing the currency, thereby enriching the Crown at the expense of his subjects, caused resentment at all levels of the community of the realm, and his policy of appeasement towards England at a time when, through the chaos of the Wars of the Roses, its southern neighbour was ripe for challenge, left him vulnerable to the manoeuvrings of the nobility. Add to that sibling rivalry. James had two younger brothers; Alexander, who was the Duke of Albany (and whom we shall henceforth refer to as Albany), and John, who was the Earl of Mar. Their older brother regarded them both as rivals, and sought to deal with them accordingly.

In John's case, in late 1479, at 22 years old, he was tried and executed. Other than paranoia on James' part, including a belief his brother had enlisted the services of a sorcerer to bring about the king's death, historians, who see John as a lamb amongst wolves, have yet to suggest a credible explanation for this fratricidal act. Albany, on the other hand was a wolf among wolves. As well as having his dukedom, he was also Warden of the Marches, a position he used, in conscious, direct opposition to his brother's appeasement policy, to sanction cross-border raids into the northern English counties. By doing so, he became the focal point of resistance to James the Anglophile, and potential rival king.

This, naturally enough, was not a state of affairs James considered he could tolerate. His response came in April 1479. It comprised a siege of Albany's seat of power, the coastal castle of Dunbar. In so far as in the following month the castle fell, the military exercise was successful. But in its principal aim – the seizure of Albany to face a charge of treason and execution upon his inevitable conviction – it failed, the duke having taken the precaution of fleeing by sea to a warm welcome in France. We'll meet up with him again in two or three years; still a wolf but, if you'll forgive the mixed metaphor, with changed spots.

To make matters worse for James, his troubles doubled when Edward's Plantagenet genes reasserted themselves, abandoning his conciliatory attitude towards the Scots and replacing it with an aggression of which the Hammer would have been proud. The reasons for this change were two-fold. Firstly, a proposed marriage, intended to cement the new found good relations between the two countries, between James' younger sister, Margaret, and an English nobleman, fell apart when she fell pregnant by her Scots lover. Secondly, although with no good corroborating evidence, Edward convinced himself James was seeking to negotiate another resurrection of the auld alliance with a view to launching an invasion of northern England as a favour to the French king, Louis XI. True, James proposed a pilgrimage to Amiens Cathedral in France – he was to be accompanied by a thousand subjects – to pay his respects to the head of John the Baptist; and true also that in anticipation of this pious act he had a gold medallion struck at the royal mint in Berwick and sent to the cathedral. Was this a threat to England? Was James hoping to meet the French king and breathe new life into the auld alliance? Probably not, but it was sufficient to persuade Edward that he should act. To combat this threat, real or imagined, he opted for belligerence – a rigorous and cruel war against the Scots, to include a pre-emptive strike unless, by way of compromise James was willing to give up his son (yes, you've guessed it, James) into Edward's custody and hand back Berwick; terms which, to no one's surprise, were rejected. War it would be, then.

Unfortunately for Edward, after leading what may without exaggeration be described as the life of a dissolute, his physical condition in the late 1470s and into the 1480s was such that while the spirit was willing the body was not. Being physically incapable of leading a military campaign, he turned instead to his brother, Richard, Duke of Gloucester, whom he charged with the twin tasks of winning Berwick back for England and bringing the Scots to heel. Neither objective, it was expected, would be easily achieved. James was immensely proud that the jewel was Scotland's once more, and he was determined to do all in his power to defend it from Gloucester's army of northern lords and their troops.

The Scottish king had invested a considerable sum from his personal resources in having the town walls and castle defences repaired and improved. Additionally, he had funded the provision of artillery and a town garrison of 500 men, whose wages were paid from his own pocket. When, in mid-1480, it was apparent to all that full hostilities between the nations were all but inevitable, the Scottish parliament, by means of demonstrating its support for the king's position, approved funding from the exchequer for the provision of a further 500 men. The parliament also took the not unfamiliar step of despatching an embassy to the king of France in the hope, sadly not realised, of breathing new life into the auld alliance.

In fact, not much happened in the first two years of the war. The Scots had a token pot shot at Bamburgh castle and indulged themselves to a modest degree in their favourite pastime of harassing the peoples of Northumberland, while for his part Gloucester led a less than determined siege of Berwick, which ended without any incident of note when, their morale sapped by the harsh Berwick winter and a lack of supplies, the besiegers headed homewards.

But the third year, 1482, was different. It starts with history repeating itself. On to our stage steps, or rather reappears after a brief exile in the wings, another would-be king of Scotland who to serve his own ambition is willing to sell the country down the river. For Edward Balliol read Albany, the Scottish king's brother, returned from France. In June 1482, the traitor entered into negotiations with Edward and Gloucester at Fotheringhay castle in Northamptonshire. What emerged from their negotiations was the Treaty of Fotheringhay, the salient terms of which were:

1.   Within two weeks of Albany making it to Edinburgh, with of course the assistance of Gloucester's army of invasion, he was to hand Berwick and its castle back in perpetuity to England; and

2   Albany was to be proclaimed king of Scotland but, *a la* Edward Balliol over two centuries before him, only as a vassal of his feudal English lord. He would be Alexander IV.

In readiness for putting the terms of the treaty into effect, Gloucester and Albany, with an army in excess of 20,000 men, arrived at Alnwick in June 1482. And Scotland's response? Well, it was not one that fills the Scottish soul with pride. While it is undoubtedly true that James was determined to carry the fight to England and defend the town, his nobles had other ideas. At Lauder in July 1482, where the Scottish host had gathered, he was taken prisoner by his own nobles and immediately thereafter transported to and incarcerated in Edinburgh castle. Whether those responsible for the coup acted out of a genuine belief that James' rule was causing the ruination of their country or, less honourably, out of the instinct for self-preservation – James may have been willing to risk life and limb in the defence of Berwick, but for others the debacle that was Halidon Hill cast a long, dark shadow – it is impossible to know.

What, however, is known is that the Scottish army dispersed. Berwick was abandoned to its fate. By the time Gloucester's army reached the south bank of the river in mid-August, anyone with any sense had already left town. Accordingly, the army found itself able to cross into and take the town unopposed. The castle was handed over on 24th August. And that was that.

For reasons explained briefly in our next chapter, the Treaty of Fotheringhay terms relating to Albany's enthronement were not observed. Instead, on James' release from imprisonment in September 1462 the Scottish king commenced a second reign, and the brothers kissed and made up.

As for Berwick, James in his renewed reign schemed and plotted to have the town returned to Scotland, but remained very much alone in holding such aspiration. More significantly for him, he retained the ability to alienate those he relied upon to keep him on his throne.

Chapter Eleven
Flowers of the Forest

Remarkably, James survived both Gloucester's post-Berwick Scottish campaign and the Lauder coup, living to reign for what in effect was a second, sadly ultimately fatal, time. The explanation for how in late September 1482 he emerged relatively unscathed from Edinburgh castle to assume full regal authority shortly thereafter is, principally, two-fold. Firstly, Gloucester ran out of time. His army reached Edinburgh on 2nd August but could only be kept in the field for a further nine days, nowhere near sufficient time to undertake a successful siege of the city's near-impregnable castle.

Secondly, if the Lauder lords were no friends of their king, they were even less well disposed towards Albany, whom they simply could not contemplate as monarch. For this reason, they were disinclined to hand over the keys of the castle to either Gloucester or Albany. James, consequently, was saved, for the time being, from regicide by being the least worst option. Gloucester headed back to England with only the return of Berwick to show for his efforts. With the upkeep of the town's garrison a cool 10,000 marks per annum, it was not necessarily a gift our fourth Edward received with particularly grateful thanks.

As for Albany, he benefited from something very close to my own heart; a little brotherly love. James, despite quite rightly knowing his brother would not stop conspiring against him, allowed Albany back into his inner circle.

In the autumn the brothers were friends again; by winter they were not, with Albany, in his Dunbar castle, in December 1482 preparing for another visit south over the border to seek assistance in tilting for the Scottish crown. His reward for his unceasing efforts to stab his brother in the back, or even in the chest, was the Treaty of Westminster, the terms of which had a familiar ring: Albany would assist Edward in conquering Scotland and cede Berwick permanently; and Edward would see Albany secure the Scottish crown (as Edward's vassal), and help him kick-start his campaign by funding 3,000 archers for six weeks. Albany's intention was to join his mate Gloucester, who was already at the border planning a land grab in the south-west of Scotland. Here we have another example of the best laid plans coming to nought, in this case as a result of our latest stage exit, that of our fourth Edward. He died, an old man at 40, body wrecked by more than good living, on 9th April 1483.

Suddenly, Gloucester's priorities had changed. Why bother playing the role of kingmaker for Albany in Scotland, why settle for the role of Lord Protector in a period of minority rule, when all he had to do to win the prize itself, the throne of England, was murder his dead brother's two young sons? The villainous, conspiring thug was content, after all, and in his own words (well, Shakespeare's, strictly speaking) to *'seem a saint, when most I play the devil.'* And devil he was. By early July, Gloucester was no longer Gloucester; he was King Richard III of England. The princes in the Tower would never see the light of day again, and in Scotland Albany was cast adrift, a hopeless pretender lacking the means to carry the fight to James. For all his conspiring, all Albany was left with was an English garrison housed at Dunbar castle, invited there as his first, and last, step in his second attempt at seizing the Scottish throne. Leaving the garrison *in situ*, he fled to England, foolishly returned to Scotland, was captured and imprisoned in Edinburgh castle, escaped by climbing down one of its walls and managed somehow to find refuge in France, where he was killed by a splinter from a lance as he was watching a jousting tournament. Unlucky. Exit another, minor, player.

In large part because of the manner of its coming into being, Richard's reign was unsettled from the outset. The first, unsuccessful, rebellion against him came as early as the autumn of 1483. For James, his second reign was, for different reasons, equally unsettled. He had learnt very little from the Lauder coup; a propensity for relying on what the nobility regarded as 'low born' confidants and for seeking to concentrate wealth in his own hands meant his position as king was almost permanently under threat from one disaffected section of the nobility or another. For these reasons, it suited the purposes of both men to reach an accord whereby neither realm was threatened by the other. Thus, following negotiations in Nottingham, at sunrise on 29th September 1484 there came into effect a truce intended to last for three years, expiring at sunset on 29th September 1487. It was a sunset Richard was destined not to see. The terms of the truce are of some interest:

1. Berwick and its castle, it was agreed, would remain unmolested by the Scots for the whole period of the truce.
2. Dunbar castle, on the other hand (still at the time in the hands of the Albany invited English garrison) could be molested provided that within six weeks of the start of the truce James gave notice of his intention to lay siege. If he gave such notice the siege could begin at any time after the first six months of the truce; if he didn't, the castle and its bounds were to be free from a Scots' attack for the full three year term.

The truce had not even reached its first anniversary, however, when all bets were off for, in August 1485, Richard exited our stage at the Battle of Bosworth, succeeded by the victor, Henry Tudor, as Henry VII. This is a significant moment for England, marking as it does the end of Plantagenet rule, and for Scotland, a kingdom no longer under threat from the Hammer's successors. The four Edwards had failed in their mission to colonise their northern neighbour, although that is not to say the Tudors (one in particular) would not cause immense problems for the country.

James, much to the chagrin of Scotland's warmongers, resisted the temptation to take advantage of the mayhem down south. His only move of any significance was the re-taking of Dunbar castle, and even that feat was not achieved until late 1485. The chroniclers are divided on whether he also ordered a siege of Berwick. If he did it was certainly unsuccessful. In general, the policy of rapprochement towards England he had pursued during the reigns of Edward number four and Richard number three was carried over into the reign of Henry number seven. Treaties and proposed marriage alliances were the order of the day. In the summer of 1486 a three year truce was agreed, in which was retained the Berwick non-molestation term, and added a further term relating to the town by which detailed arrangements were put in place to determine its bounds. Throughout the first eighteen months of this accord, negotiations continued for its renewal and extension; and it was to be underpinned, the Scots proposed, by no fewer than three royal marriages between the Stewarts and what was left of the house of York. James (a recent widower) was to be wed to Elizabeth, widow of Edward number four, and his two sons were to be married to daughters of the late English king. It is difficult to believe these suggested marriages were looked upon with any enthusiasm in England by the new Tudors or the Lancastrian rump, out of power but still lurking in the background. It mattered not, however, for James' second reign was about to come to an abrupt, violent end.

On 11th June 1488, with Robert's 1314 Battle of Bannockburn sword in hand, James died in battle, at Bannockburn. Over the years, so as to distinguish between the two encounters, the battle in which James lost his life became, and remains, known as the Battle of Sauchieburn. It represented another example of the Scots' ability to wage war amongst their own; and as the leader of the regicidal rebels was none other than James' fifteen-year-old son – bid a warm welcome to James number four – a very long shadow was cast over the early years of the new, young king's reign.

In the early years, the one and only priority for our new James was to secure his kingship, an ambition he would be better able to concentrate upon if the threat of invasion could be avoided. In the first instance, therefore, he followed in his father's appeasing footsteps. Despite the final truce between Scotland and England negotiated by the late king ending in September 1489, our fourth James did his utmost to ensure friendly relations between the two countries continued. Those efforts led to a five year treaty negotiated in 1491, and finalised at Coldstream, the terms of which were similar to the treaties entered into under our third James' reign. By my reckoning, the 1491 treaty was the first of six treaties or treaty extensions culminating at the start of the sixteenth century in the Treaty of Perpetual Peace. What distinguished this one from all its fifteenth century predecessors was that the marriage alliance it envisaged actually went ahead; at Holyrood in August 1503 James married Margaret Tudor, daughter of the reigning English king, Henry number seven, and sister to the prince who in due course became number eight of that name.

This, with thanks to Ridpath, is what the treaty had to say about Berwick and its castle:

'That these, with their ancient bounds and the inhabitants thereof, should forever remain and be included in the present perpetual peace, friendship, league, and confederacy; so that neither the king of Scotland, his heirs or successors, nor any of them should, by themselves , or any of their subjects, lieges, or vassals, make or suffer to be made, war, insult, ambush, or siege, publicly or privately, against the places themselves or their inhabitants; nor the king of England, his heirs, successors, or any of them, should by themselves, or the inhabitants of the town and castle, make any war, insult, or siege, on the king of Scotland or his vassals.'

A new century; a new dawn; peace in perpetuity? Not a chance. The signs that little would change were there for all to see even before the treaty had been signed. In the previous decade, the several peace treaties notwithstanding, James had proved to be something of an opportunist, and was considered – quite rightly – by those on the south side of the border as untrustworthy. He had, after all, allowed Perkin Warbeck to set up home in Scotland and marry into the kingdom's aristocracy. For the record, Warbeck claimed he was Prince Richard, the youngest son of Edward IV, and the rightful king of England; rumours he had perished in the Tower of London being demonstrably untrue. Nonsense though the impostor's claims were, it suited James' purpose to appear to believe them, for a short time at least, just to keep Henry on his toes.

And that is precisely what the English king did. In late 1497 he received parliamentary approval to raise a tax to fund an army of invasion, only to be distracted by stirrings of rebellion in Cornwall. Seeing this as an opportune moment to go on the offensive, James launched an old-fashioned raid into northern England and laid an unsuccessful siege of Norham castle, the defence of which was ably managed by the Bishop of Durham. When Henry's army eventually headed northwards, the Scots re-crossed the border. The pursuing army also crossed but had taken only Ayton castle into its possession before diplomacy brought the nascent conflict to an end.

The Stewart–Tudor marriage alliance changed little, if anything at all. Son-in-law and father-in-law remained mistrustful of each other. James believed Henry was looking for signs of weakness in the Scots with a view to embarking on a campaign similar to the Gloucester led invasion of 1482; Henry was convinced, and was right in being so, that James only had eyes for France and was looking to renew the auld alliance on terms favourable to him. The tension generated by this mutual suspicion manifested itself twice in Berwick; firstly, in 1505 when the fighting men of Northumberland were called upon to be in readiness to defend the town against an expected Scottish onslaught; and secondly in

1508 when the town's garrison was increased, skilled masons employed to undertake repairs to the walls, and the good folk of Berwick encouraged to practise a little self-help by digging defensive ditches.

But, albeit precariously, the peace part of the treaty survived its early years; Berwick was neither besieged by the Scots nor used as a base camp for yet another English invasion of Scotland. Had it not been for our next exit and melodramatic entrance the perpetual part might have been realised, with James becoming the model son-in-law for whom any father-in-law could wish. Henry, in April 1509, gives us our exit; his eighteen year old son, Henry number eight, is our new entrant and provides the melodrama. I'm Henry the Eighth he proclaimed, I am, I am, and not only am I king of England I'm also overlord of Scotland and king of France. Though a Tudor, he was (maybe with the exception of the feckless Edward II and insane Henry VI) all the Plantagenets rolled into one. It took him a while to get going, for he was three years into his reign when his army first crossed to Europe, and it was another year later before, at the end of June 1513, he set sail for France, when his campaign (which was doomed from the outset but that is another story) to be crowned in Paris began in earnest.

Henry, being his father's son, was of course brother-in-law to James and brother of the queen of Scotland, his older sister, Margaret. Not that any of this mattered; he was no more willing to recognise Scotland's independence than were his Plantagenet predecessors; Scotland would be his, after he had dealt with France.

Henry's hubristic belligerence towards France was just what James needed to strengthen his hand in having new life breathed into the auld alliance. Not for the first time history was repeating itself; following the same train of thought as his forebears, the French king, Louis XII (that's the twelfth, so be thankful the kings Louis don't appear too often in our tale) concluded that a threat to England's northern border, and even better an invasion, would assist his cause by requiring Henry to divide his forces between attack in France and defence in northern counties of

England. Money aplenty, supplies, weapons and military advisers were offered to and accepted by James; the auld alliance was once more, and the French king had good reason to believe it would work in his favour, for James, in the years from 1502, had gone about systematically building up Scotland's military capability, having a particular penchant for acquiring the latest in heavy artillery and building the largest battleships contemporary technology would allow. By 1513 he was ready for war, and with Henry safely out of the way on French soil he saw the perfect opportunity, in the 25th year of his reign, to establish himself as a European monarch to be reckoned with and respected.

In the last week of July, the love of James' life – his navy – set sail for the Channel, intending to join up with the French. Together, the two navies would prevent Henry and his army from re-crossing to England once his vainglorious enterprise had been seen off. These days, navies are funded and maintained from the public purse. That was not the case in the sixteenth century when, for the most part, ships including those armed for battle, were in private hands and, with their crews, hired out to the sovereign only when needed. But James was different; from an early age he showed a deep interest in creating a fleet, paid for either in significant part or wholly from Crown revenues, to be placed under his control and to complement privately supplied vessels. Thus, the fleet that headed towards the Channel was led by three ships of majestic size and design, all commissioned by James; they were the 'Michael', the 'James' and the 'Margaret'. Of the three it was the 'Michael' which was James' pride and joy. It was a truly magnificent specimen for its time; built at a cost of £30,000, weighing perhaps 1,000 tons and 180 feet long, with 27 cannon and a generous supply of smaller artillery, as well as the more traditional form of weaponry, crossbows and longbows, it matched and even surpassed the best Henry could offer, including the Mary Rose. It would prove a valuable asset to the French, though not in the way envisaged by James.

The Scottish army of invasion was an equally impressive force. The largest army ever to cross the border, it was armed with the most up to date heavy artillery, not least of which were cannon forged within the walls of Edinburgh castle, the famous 'Seven Sisters', each of them having to be transported by the combined strength of 36 oxen. All that was missing from this impressive array – too large to be drawn into England – was Mons Meg.

Not that the campaign got off to the best of starts for the Scots. An initial raid into Northumberland for plunder turned into a disaster for them when 400 to 500 of their number were killed in an ambush by a small English force on the flat, Milfield plain. It came, with obvious good reason, to be known as the 'Ill Raid'. But it had no deterrent effect. And so it was that on or about 22nd August 1513, James, Scotland's most charismatic king since the Bruce, led his troops over the Tweed at Coldstream, into England. It was then that the rain started. Two or so weeks later, in the late afternoon of 9th September, the opposing armies of England and Scotland confronted each other, a few hundred yards apart on Flodden Field. And it was still raining. And added to the rain was a wind so strong that it rendered the English archers redundant in battle for the first time in 200 years, and mud so thick that as the Scots advanced downhill at the commencement of the battle they removed their boots in the vain hope of gaining a better grip in the ground beneath their feet.

Myth has it that James had been forewarned. A few days before the invasion, while in prayer for the success of his campaign, an apparition, said to have been in the form of a man with shoulder-length yellow hair and dressed in a blue gown, warned James that should he dally with the opposite sex he would lead his army to disaster and himself to shame; just as a shaken bush loses its leaves in the autumn wind, so Scotland's finest would fall in battle. Yet James, it seemed, had no need to heed the warning. He stood at the head of an army 30,000 strong, an army in many respects the most technologically advanced in Europe.

For the Scots, once they had crossed the border, all seemed to be falling nicely into place. Norham castle, which had been an English border stronghold for centuries, fell after six days of pummelling by Scottish cannon. Etal, Wark and Ford castles quickly followed. Berwick, little more than a garrison town since last falling into English hands in 1482, was poorly defended and obviously vulnerable. However, ignoring advice to take the town and consolidate his position by means of a mundane siege, James instead sought the glory of battle. Eager to confront the English, Berwick could wait until his triumphant return.

Life, though, was comfortable, a little too comfortable, at Ford castle where James enjoyed the company of the lady of the house and her daughter. While James dallied, hearing but ignoring the blue gowned augur whispering in his ear, and his army sat on its heels, the English forces, led by the Earl of Surrey, moved north. By 4th September they had reached Alnwick, causing James to at last rise from his slumbers. On 5th September, James' army occupied the high ground of Flodden Edge, as secure a defensive position as can be imagined. This is how it is described in the chronicles:

> *'The King lay upon the edge of a mountain, called Flodden, on the edge of the Cheviot, where [there] was but one narrow field for any man to ascend up the said hill to him, and at the foot of the hill lay all his ordinance. On the one side of his army was a great marsh, and compassed with the hills of Cheviot, so that he lay too strong to be approached of any side, except that the Englishmen would have temerariously run on his ordinance.'* (Niall Barr, *'Flodden'* p.105, quoting from Edward Hall's *'The Triumphant Reigne of Kyng Henry VIII'* volume I).

But Surrey was no timorous wee beastie, nor was he foolish enough to contemplate ordering his fighting men to run uphill headlong into artillery fire. What is more, he and James had history; it was Surrey who had led the relief of Norham castle in 1497 in response to James' first, failed, attempt to seize it. Surrey continued advancing north-wards, stopping for short periods at Newcastle and Alnwick, and on 8th September reaching Barmour castle, north of Wooler. Momentum was gathering. Surrey was determined James would have his battle, but not on the terms the king of Scots envisaged.

On the morning of 9th September the English army set off on a march which took it north from Barmour towards Cornhill, past the watching Scots and causing uncertainty in their camp. Was Surrey taking his army to Berwick for re-provisioning, or into Scotland as an invading force, or to the only available position – Branxton Hill – from which an attack on the Scots army could conceivably be launched? The answer came when the English vanguard reached Twizell Bridge, crossed it and marched south towards Branxton. All of this was watched with intense interest by the Scottish scouts and reported back to James, who reacted by having his army reposition itself and regroup on Branxton Hill. No advantage appeared to have been lost by this manoeuvre; if anything the Scots were now in a stronger position, having beaten Surrey to the only high ground that would have been of any benefit to him. To attack the Scots, his troops would have to charge uphill – it would be Halidon Hill with roles reversed. Only it wasn't, except in the sense that the Scots charged downhill rather than uphill to defeat.

The wind and rain that had greeted the Scottish invasion continued unabated as the two armies faced each other. The conditions were such that the weapon which for centuries had been central to English successes in battle, the longbow, was made redundant. Modernity stepped into the vacuum; the early exchanges at Flodden were artil-lery exchanges, Scottish heavy cannon pitted against lighter English pieces. The outcome was the Seven Sisters were second best. Loading, firing, recoiling several feet and having to be moved back into posi-tion after firing for the process to recommence, the Scottish cannon were too ponderous to be effective against English weapons which could be fired, re-loaded and fired again with relative rapidity. The four or five phalanxes of stationary Scots troops at the top of Branxton Hill were sitting ducks, and in those circumstances James had only two realistic options; either take his army out of sight and range by moving it back over the crest of the hill or ordering an attack. Shortly after four o'clock in the afternoon, he chose option two, ordering a charge down the steep slope of the hill into the waiting English ranks. But the ground beneath the advancing Scots was sodden and marshy, and worse was to come when they came across, entirely unexpectedly, a rain bloated burn at the bottom of the hill. In crossing the burn, the Scots lost their carefully choreographed formation, never to regain it, before reaching the waiting English. It was at that point that, despite the close-quarter fighting continuing for most of the rest of the day, the battle was lost and won.

Lessons in Scottish warfare no.2

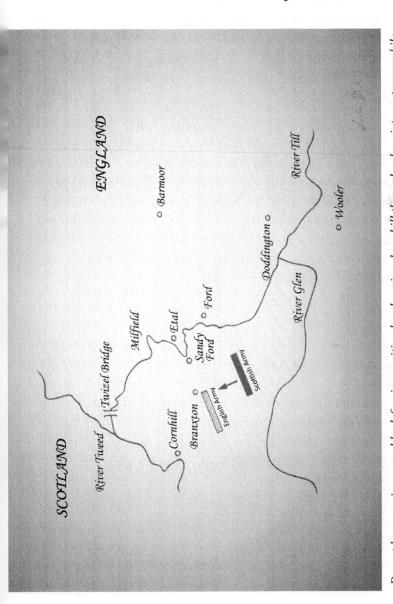

Do not leave an impregnable defensive position by charging downhill through a bog into a stream while facing heavy artillery fire and expect to win the day. As the Scottish army, having left the safety of Flodden Edge for Branxton Hill, descended towards the stationary English troops, it lost formation on crossing a rain bloated burn at the foot of the hill, James being hacked to death in the ensuing chaos of battle.

Darkness had fallen by the time the fighting ended. The following morning the English were able to declare themselves the victors, though even then skirmishes broke out sporadically. Thousands, many more Scots than English, had been killed. They were buried together, united in death, in mass graves on land to the south-west of the battlefield.

What became of James? The answer depends very much upon whether you prefer a second Flodden myth or the historical record. The latter has it that James was killed in battle. His mutilated body was identified in the early morning light of the day after the battle, taken to a Berwick church where it lay for several days before being transported first to Newcastle, then to London and finally to Richmond where it was lost to history, never to enjoy the dignity of a proper burial. Myth, however, will not countenance the possibility that James might have fallen in battle or acquiesce in the shameful treatment of his remains in death. No, James did not fall. He was rescued from the battlefield by four, biblically inspired, horsemen who appeared in the midst of the battle to spirit him away through the flailing weapons of the English billmen to the safety of Scotland.

For those who did fall, they lie, the flowers of the forest, at peace in the tranquil countryside of north Northumberland. As the lament tells:

Dule and wae for the order, sent oor lads to the Border
The English, for aince, by guile wan the day
The Flooers of the Forest, that focht aye the foremost
The prime o our land, lie cauld in the clay.

Flodden was the last of the battles fought near or for Berwick. While it would be several centuries hence before a lasting peace between the two warring nations of England and Scotland finally broke out, the town, albeit of central importance as a defensive stronghold during the Tudor period, would no longer find itself at the epicentre of the conflict.

Flodden is fifteen miles from Berwick, and ought to be visited. The battle site is a tranquil place, movingly marked by a plain stone cross, erected in 1910, dedicated to the brave of both nations.

A footnote. Don't think Flodden represented a simple confrontation between two nations. There were other forces at play. The site of the battle was in reiver land, the lawless frontier land where neither nation was able to enforce any significant degree of control over the populace, where families and communities were bound together by name, recognising no jurisdiction except their own. They were the banditti, their survival dependent on the success of their raiding parties. And they remind us the past is not so very far behind. Just pause for a moment or two and you'll realise they are still with us. They are recognisable to Berwick folk by their surnames – Anderson, Bell, Dalgliesh, Dickson, Elliot, Forster, Graham, Gray, Paul, Henderson, Hunter, Laidlaw, Louther, Maxwell, Oliver, Redpath, Rutherford, Scott, Tait, Turnbull, Wilkinson, and Young; and they're only the ones I went to school with. All are reiver names, linked you may be sure back through the centuries to Flodden. Some of their ancestors will have fought for the Scots, some for the English, but still others, perhaps even the majority, for the name only, with no thought of nation or nationhood.

Chapter Twelve
No Entry:
Scots and French Keep Out

If Flodden Field was the last of the great battles fought near or for Berwick, it did not by any means signify the end of the Anglo-Scottish wars. For most of the remainder of the sixteenth century such was the fear in England of an auld alliance invasion of Scots and French from the north that Henry number eight, followed by his three immediate successors, expended vast sums on improving the town's defences, culminating in what we see before us today, the Elizabethan Walls – the Walls, as we shall mostly refer to them hereinafter.

James number four was succeeded after Flodden by his toddler son, James number five, whose reign, for the purposes of our story, was largely unremarkable. Berwick was undisturbed, so much so that it became the appointed meeting place for the holding of treaty negotiations between commissioners of Scotland and England. Innumerable peace agreements, some lasting only several months, others, in theory, several years, were entered into but generally honoured more in the breach than the observance; it was during James number five's reign that Berwick's border town cousins, Jedburgh and Kelso (and their abbeys), and Coldingham suffered terribly at the hands of Henry's henchmen. Of these peace treaties, it is the last of them, or to be more precise a related, supplemental agreement to it, that is of most interest to us. In May 1534 a treaty between the two kingdoms was concluded with the intention that it would remain in place during the joint lives of the two kings and for a whole year after the death of the first of them.

It was breached regularly by both sides and at one stage, in 1542 just a few weeks before James' death – he predeceased Henry by five years – open warfare was once again on the cards until the Scottish nobility, with the Flodden wipe out in mind, sent a sick note to James; they were, they explained, suffering from a sudden attack of *frigidi pedes*. James died a few weeks later, of a broken heart it was rumoured at the time. Cholera was a more likely candidate.

By the 1534 supplemental agreement terms, Henry had promised to return to James a house (possibly it was a fortress) on the north side of the border at Eddrington that had been in English possession for several decades. Ridpath tells us the agreement contained a clause relating specifically to Berwick which was found in all of the post-1482 treaties between the two kingdoms. The clause in question was:

Per dictum illustrissimum regem anglia vassalos sive subditos regni aut inhabitants nullam & castrum Berwice quoscumque

Yes, you're right, it's written in Latin. What it means, in terms of the Eddrington agreement, is that the residents thereof would be molested neither by the subjects of the illustrious king of England nor the inhabitants of the town or castle of Berwick. The express reference to Berwick in the clause is of the highest significance, as, to borrow from Ridpath:

'This favours the idea, suggested by the whole series of treaties concluded since the recovery of Berwick by the English, in the end of the reign of Edward IV [i.e. in 1482], that Berwick was not considered as a part of the realm of England.'

The idea of the constitutional position of Berwick being in English possession and under its control but at the same time not a part of England is a subject to which we shall return in Chapter Thirteen. For the moment, let's get back to the Walls.

Upon James exiting stage left on 14th December 1542 he was replaced stage right by his week-old daughter, the queen we all know and love, the voluptuous Mary Queen of Scots. Save to mention that the Scots resisted Henry's rough wooing attempts to marry her off to his son, Edward, by finding safe haven for her in the French royal court, we skip over the first seventeen years of Mary's life (during which time three English monarchs exit our stage, Henry, Mary I and Edward VI) to find her, through marriage, becoming Queen Consort of France on her dauphin husband, Francis, succeeding to the French throne on 10th July 1559. Watching this momentous event with some trepidation from across the Channel was Elizabeth I of England, in the first year of her reign. And there, in a nutshell, is the reason for the Walls coming into being.

A little explanation is required. Throughout Mary Stuart's early years the fear of an auld alliance invasion of England troubled first Henry, then his son, Edward VI and then his daughter, the English Mary Tudor when she became Mary I, to a degree sufficient for them to put in place plans, some realised, some not, to extend and improve Berwick's defences. But, suddenly, in the marriage of the French and Scottish royal houses and in particular in the person of our Scottish Mary, who arguably had as good a claim to the crown of England as her cousin once removed, the perceived threat to Elizabeth increased exponentially – for Mary Queen of Scots think instead of Mary Stuart, Queen of Scotland, France and England.

Just a little genealogy to clarify the point:

Mary

We start with Henry number seven. Remember, his daughter, Margaret, married James number four of Scotland. Their son was James number five and his daughter, Mary Stuart, aka Mary Queen of Scots was, consequently, the legitimate great granddaughter of Henry number seven of England. She also happened to be a Roman Catholic.

Elizabeth

Henry number seven's first son was Arthur. At the grand old age of thirteen, Arthur was married by proxy to Catherine of Aragon, who at fourteen was even older than her husband, and living in Spain at the date of the marriage. In 1509, Catherine travelled to England where Arthur and she were married in a second wedding ceremony, on which occasion both were present. Four months later Arthur exited. Stepping into comfort by way of marriage the widowed Catherine, was number seven's second eldest son, Henry number eight in waiting.

All was fine and dandy in the marriage for quite a considerable period of time, until Catherine's husband fell for the charms of Anne Boleyn, a match which set in motion in the world of religion a chain of events so seismic the shockwaves are still felt in our time. In a sentence, to facilitate his marriage to Anne, Henry broke with Catholic Rome (although ironically to his dying day he remained a practising Catholic), had himself declared supreme Head of the Church in England and, thereby, in May 1533 was able to have his twenty plus years marriage to Catherine annulled; that is to say, declared null and void from the outset.

And there lay the problem for Elizabeth, aka the Virgin Queen, aka Good Queen Bess. She was the child of the marriage of Henry and Anne, a union not recognised by most of the rest of Europe or a very sizeable proportion of Catholics in England. Their reasoning was straightforward enough; Henry's annulment of his marriage to Catherine was not lawful, and it therefore followed his marriage to Anne was not lawful, and it therefore followed Elizabeth was illegitimate. By the laws of the land at the time, an illegitimate child could not assume the throne, thus meaning Mary Queen of Scots as the legitimate great granddaughter of Henry number seven had a better claim to the English crown than

Elizabeth, his illegitimate, bastard grandchild.

Make no mistake; there was force in this argument, enough to make Elizabeth rightly extremely nervous of a challenge to her throne from her Scottish cousin. If there was going to be a Franco-Scots invasion, it would, most likely, commence in the eastern march. Consequently, as a purely defensive measure, Elizabeth resolved to spare no expense in making Berwick impregnable. The Walls were summoned into existence.

If you would like to learn a lot about the Walls in a short period of time you can do no better than read the 30 pages of excellent description, explanation and comment in the form of Iain MacIvor's *'Fortifications of Berwick-upon-Tweed'* (1983) and, if you can get hold of a copy, Reverend James King's *'The Edwardian Walls and Elizabethan Ramparts of Berwick-upon-Tweed'* (1906). My grateful thanks to both men, because much of what follows is based on their articles.

The design and construction of the Walls are largely the work of two men, who did not always see eye to eye. First to be appointed, in January 1558, was the English military engineer, Sir Richard Lee. Not long afterwards, and not necessarily to Lee's liking, an Italian engineer, Giovanni Portinari, was drafted in to lend support and, in fact, what we see today – a bastioned defence known as the 'Italian System' (a forerunner, experts believe, of the Helinio Herrera catenaccio system of defence swept aside by a twentieth century Scottish whirlwind) – is much more Portinari than Lee.

Work commenced in or around 1560, all involved being in agreement that the Edwardian walls to the north should be abandoned, as it would be too expensive to rebuild them and in any case that part of the town was sparsely populated, and replaced with entirely new walls, a quarter of a mile or thereabouts nearer the town centre. Also, and again uncontroversially, it was decided the castle, which to a great extent had fallen into disuse, would be left outside the new walls. Have a look at my good friend Laszlo's pencil drawing on page 151. It is taken from

John Speed's 1624 map of Northumberland and inset of Berwick town. You can easily see the castle (now the railway station) and the line of the Edwardian walls, or what was left of them by 1624, running from the north-eastern corner of the castle to what is now known as Lord's Mount. Inside that line, the replacement northern section of new Walls, more or less just as we see it today, starts at Meg's Mount and ends at the Brass Bastion.

Reverend King makes the entirely reasonable point that much of the masonry of the old walls was likely to have been recycled in the construction of the new walls. When you're walking around them (Ryan's Guided Tours follows on pages 136–150) look out for large square-cut sandstone stones varying in colour from white to deep red. If you spot any, more likely than not you are looking at a Plantagenet, not Tudor, legacy.

A 'bastion', MacIvor tells us, is the strongpoint of an artillery fortification, corresponding to the towers of a medieval castle or town hall. Reverend King gives a more precise definition – *'a projecting pentagonal fort, placed at an angle of a fortification'*. The Walls have five bastions, though in some cases you'll have more than a little difficulty identifying their pentangular shape, namely: Meg's Mount; Cumberland Bastion; Brass Bastion; Windmill Bastion; and King's Mount.

At a cost of £128,848, five shillings and nine-and-a-half pence, by the close of 1566 the masonry construction work on the Walls was complete. The project was the single most costly capital undertaking of Elizabeth's reign. The earthen mounds, giving the Walls their appearance as we see them today, were added in later years. Surrounding the Walls was a ditch 200 feet wide, in the middle of which was a trench twelve feet wide and eight feet deep filled with water.

At the commencement of the works, it had been Lee's intention that the five bastions would be similar in design, but, over the six or so years of their construction, compromises, some dictated by the practical considerations the engineers encountered as they went along and others by financial constraints, meant the finished article was not quite as envisaged at the outset.

There is, I know you will agree, no better way to appreciate the Elizabethan Walls and their Plantagenet forebears than by partaking in a modest amount of exercise of the type all of us in these isles know and love, the circular walk, with the occasional detour. To ensure you don't get lost, in addition to having me as your guide, you have not one but two maps to rely upon. The first on page 144 is Laszlo's pencil drawing of one of the plans found in MacIvor's article, and the other, on page 151, is Laszlo's drawing of John Speed's town plan. Though for the purposes of the walks I've only bothered to number MacIvor's plan, you'll have no difficulty following them on Speed's town plan if you prefer.

We assemble at the junction of West Street and Bridge Street (1), where we immediately face a dilemma; do we start now or do we first have a pint in Barrels opposite? Dilemma resolved (either way, I don't mind), from the junction, as we look towards the Old Bridge, a right turn takes us into Love Lane. After 200 yards, at the foot of Bank Hill (2) a second dilemma awaits, being a choice of routes, because, unless you can defy the laws of physics, you have to choose between The Kings' Walk – Part One and The Queen's Walk, though whichever you choose you will end up on the same final short stretch, being the Kings' Walk – Part Two. Note the apostrophes: after the 's' in Kings' because at least five were responsible for the medieval walls – the Hammer, his son Edward number two, Robert, Henry number eight, and his son and successor, Edward VI – and several others for the construction and enlargement of the castle, David I of Scotland and the first three Henrys of England among them; and before the 's' in Queen's because we give credit for the construction of the Walls only to one monarch, Tudor Elizabeth. Here we go then.

The Kings' Walk – Part One

At the bottom of Bank Hill (2 on the plan), we keep to the left of the stone pillar, walking along the riverside and under the road bridge. With the Berwick Amateur Rowing Club boat house on our left, we enter Castle Vale Park, following the path sign posted 'Riverside Walk'. To local folk, Riverside Walk is known as the New Road. Walking along, we are following on our right the line of the medieval walls, the bequest of, principally but not exclusively, our otherwise inept second Edward (yes, that's right, the one who lost at Bannockburn). Don't, though, be misled; the masonry you see through the trees is not 700 years old. Most if not all of this section was rebuilt in the eighteenth century, the medieval walls having by then been in a state of ruin for several centuries. The Walls are hidden from sight by a bank of trees, which is a shame. If King is right, a part of this section, though what if anything remains of it, it is well-nigh impossible to say, was originally built on Robert's orders.

Two or three minutes' walk along New Road brings us to what is left of the castle. We enter it through a low, narrow passage (K1) below the remains of a gun tower, and on our right rising up the hill towards the railway station is the White Wall/Breakneck Stairs. The wall along the crest of the hill is the same wall you can see, naturally from the other side, from Platform 2 of the railway station. But there is more of the castle left than what you see on the hill. Turn around. Before you is the castle in a different guise, that of Robert Stephenson's viaduct, the Royal Border Bridge. It is one of the countless triumphs of the Industrial Revolution. Was, however, its construction an act of vandalism? Frederick Sheldon tells us that in 1844 a parliamentary bill was passed for the building of a railway between Edinburgh and Berwick, with the station in our gude town to be sited on Castle Hill, and with the demolition of the castle a necessary consequence.

And it made common and commercial sense to recycle the castle's masonry in the construction of the bridge that was to link Scotland to

England. It was, nevertheless, a cause for regret. The castle had stood proudly on the north bank of the Tweed for 700 years, but now, seeing the history within its walls swept aside for the sake of progress, Sheldon pines '....*the last blow must be given to the old Castle, the deadliest of all its wounds; others have feloniously appropriated its stones to sacred and warlike purposes, pillaged its riches, but still left something; but this attack is complete deracination.'*

In 1846, for 3s 6d a day, Scots, Irish and English drengs and navvies were let loose. Within four years the castle was no more and the bridge had come magnificently into being, as one observer put it, hanging in the air halfway between the Tweed and the clouds.

Continuing through the passage, several hundred yards on we reach a footpath sign posted 'Coronation Park' (K2). Walking up the meandering path, there are wonderful views of the river, the railway bridge, and the castle's remains. On reaching Coronation Park, the short path on our left takes us up on to the main road, just on the north side of the road bridge that crosses the main east coast railway line. Cross the road and turn right over the bridge towards town. On our left immediately after crossing is Northumberland Avenue, which is where we're heading. However, if you feel like taking a short detour, a visit to the railway station opposite for two or three minutes is all that is needed to see the plaque commemorating John Balliol's success in the Great Cause and to have a look from Platform 2 at what is left of the castle wall.

After walking along Northumberland Avenue and past the old grammar school, we see a ditch and earthen bank. Not much to look at, I grant you, for we non-archaeologists, but here is history; this is the Hammer's handiwork, seeking to improve the town's defences after the 1296 massacre. The Bell Tower (K3) also dates from the same period, though much of it was rebuilt in Tudor times. The footpath adjacent to the tower takes us across the ditch into Low Greens. Just in time for a break, a left turn leads us to the Pilot. I had my first ever pint in the Pilot – of McEwan's Tartan – and several more, fifteen years old on the way to a fifth form school dance at the grammar school. Not a moment worth reflecting on at length, except for me I suppose.

Left out of the Pilot, and 50 yards or so on, another left turn along a short footpath takes us forward in time. In the space of less than a quarter of a mile from the Hammer's ditch, we've travelled two and a half centuries, for here is Lord's Mount (K4), bequeathed to us by the promiscuous, adulterous, six times married Henry number eight. Built on the site of a pre-existing earthen bulwark, between 1539 and 1542 a circular masonry fort having a diameter of 100 feet and walls nineteen feet thick was constructed. It was intended that the fort would protect a weak spot in the Edwardian fortifications, vulnerable to attack on two sides, from the north and from the east across Magdalene Fields. The fort has been excellently excavated and rewards exploration.

250 years in 250 yards

A view of Bell Tower from inside Lord's Mount – our eighth Henry looking two-and-a-half centuries back in time to Edwards one and two.

On leaving Lord's Mount, we take the small set of railed steps down on to the path. Turning left, after just a few yards we find ourselves on a footpath heading towards Cowport. On our left is Magdalene Fields Golf Course and on our right are some further remnants of the Edwardian walls (K5). Continuing along the footpath, we have our first sight of the Elizabethan Walls in the form of Brass Bastion and, bisecting the golf course in the direction of the coast, the traverse known as the 'Covered Way' also soon comes into view. For details of both see the Queen's Walk. At this point the path joins a narrow tarmac road skirting a place still close to my heart, The Stanks football pitch, and heading in towards the town through Cowport. The gate is Elizabethan, built at the same time as the Walls and therefore, just to confuse you, it has a 'Q' number – Q5. A sharp uphill turn through an iron gate just as we've passed through Cowport takes us on to Elizabeth's Walls. Taking a right turn at the top of the path, we join the Queen's Walk heading towards Windmill Bastion. Now turn to page 147 and follow the walk from Cowport. It won't be long before you rejoin the Kings' Walk.

The Queen's Walk

From the foot of Bank Hill (2), we walk steeply upwards, passing under the arches of the road bridge. If the quarter-mile walk from Barrels has left you exhausted and weary limbed you can always take a right turn near the top of the hill for a well-deserved drink in The Leaping Salmon. Fifty yards farther up the hill we're there, on the Walls, at the foot of Meg's Mount (Q1), and this is where we stop for a few minutes, to learn a bit about the terminology used to describe their various features, courtesy of King and MacIvor.

Cavalier

King – literally, *a horseman* – a huge mound raised on the central position of the terreplein of a bastion, from the top of which guns are fired over the lower batteries, as a horseman can fire over infantry.

MacIvor – a gun platform raised above the level of a bastion or curtain to improve the field of fire.

Curtain

King – (Lat. *Cortina,* a small court) the part of a rampart extending between two bastions, forming with the flanks a sort of court or enclosed area.

MacIvor – the length of rampart between two bastions.

Face

MacIvor only –The straight sides of a bastion towards the field, meeting in a point, are called the faces. They give all varieties of the bastion plan a characteristic angular shape.

Flank

King – the side of a bastion reaching from the face to the curtain commanding the main ditch and the face of the opposite bastion.

McIvor – the faces of a bastion are joined to the curtains by the flanks.

Flanker

King – large, open, rectangular courts of masonry, found in the Berwick ramparts.

MacIvor – a gun emplacement recessed into the flank of a bastion.

Terreplein

King – the top level part of a rampart or bastion on which cannon are placed.

McIvor – the broad level fighting-platform of bastions and curtains behind the parapets.

Now that we're experts in the field of military architecture, we can have a look at Meg's Mount. It is where work on the Walls started, and where the first construction compromise was made. As you see, it is really only a half-bastion, or if you prefer a demi-bastion. It has two faces, one looking over the river, and the other facing north towards Scotland. But it has only one flank and, consequently, one flanker. Standing at the top of the cavalier you're about 150 feet above the Tweed, where you have a view of the Cheviots to the south and the Eildon Hills to the west. A nicely balanced, even-handed poem for you, (from King):

Southwards spreads fair England smiling,
To the west the Eildon Hills blue;
While northward, ever hearts beguiling,
Lies old Scotland, brave and true.

Royal walks

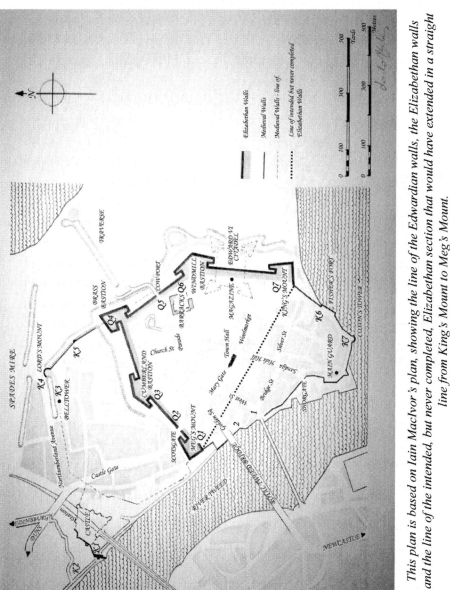

This plan is based on Iain MacIvor's plan, showing the line of the Edwardian walls, the Elizabethan walls and the line of the intended, but never completed, Elizabethan section that would have extended in a straight line from King's Mount to Meg's Mount.

Leaving Meg's Mount and heading towards Cumberland Bastion, we have a choice of paths. The higher of the two gives the best views. The lower path is at the level of the terreplein. Both paths were laid in 1837, when the Walls became a tourist attraction. Not more than a hundred yards on from Meg's Mount, we walk over the Scotsgate arch (Q2). Look north, not now, when it was first built, and you see the barbarians, in this instance the Scots, knocking on Heaven's door, determined to re-enter Paradise; look south, not now but then, and you see a militarised town, waiting for the onslaught to begin. These days, thanks to the widening of the arch in 1815 and 1858, the old A1 passes underneath, just about wide enough if you breathe in to allow two cars to pass. Back then, it was like the Cowport gate was and still is; if the Scots were going to come through they would have to do so in single file.

A short distance on from Scotsgate, to our right is Wallace Green, where, somewhere, lie the remains of the Wallace. As you pass, Sheldon will be watching you, so be sure to reverentially doff your bonnet.

Next stop is the whole point of the exercise, a complete, regular bastion, namely, depending on your preference, Middle Bastion or Cumberland Bastion (Q3), after the Duke of Cumberland credited with the defeat of Bonnie Prince Charlie at the battle of Culloden in 1745, a date outwith the parameters of our story, and thus another (yet another) Scots' defeat we can quickly draw a veil over.

At Cumberland Bastion, the rationale behind the Italian defensive system may be clearly seen. On top of the masonry wall is an earthworks parapet and within there is a raised central platform, a cavalier. Cannon were placed at both parapet and cavalier level, and additionally within the two flankers westwards facing towards the Meg's Mount flanker and eastwards towards Brass Bastion's western flanker. In this way, the northern face of the Walls could be given maximum protection by fire and cross-fire. King says if we look eastwards from Cumberland we can see the ditch and trench within it running from Cumberland to Bastion. All that is missing, though you have to use your imagination

145

to see the ditch, is the water that in Elizabethan times would have filled the trench.

Have a look at the illustration on page 144. You'll see that the design of Brass Bastion (Q4), our next stop, is anything but regular. With its two flankers, it is entitled to be regarded as a full bastion, but the angle of its eastern wall had to be distorted from what was originally intended so as to bring it into alignment with the line of the Walls leading to Windmill Bastion. The construction of Brass was one of the few instances when Portinari did not get his way. Had he done so, the Walls would be an even more impressive sight. To further protect the town from attack from the north or by sea, Portinari planned to continue the construction of the Walls eastwards from Brass Bastion all the way to the coast, down to what is now Pier Road, and then back inland to King's Mount (Q7). He was outvoted, on grounds of expense. Instead, a significantly less expensive alternative was adopted. Just to the south of Brass a deep ditch, running east-west, known as the 'Covered Way', was dug. What remains of it can be easily seen from the top of the Brass cavalier. It bisects the municipal golf course, and is marked on our plan as the 'Traverse'.

Walking along the footpath from Brass towards Windmill Bastion, down below on the left is my nomination for recognition as a World Heritage Site, the Stanks football pitch. The pitch, I agree, is not the oldest in the world, and I realise some poor obsessive compulsive soul will delight in contradicting me, but surely the two sides of the ground comprising, firstly, the curtain wall between Brass and Cowport (Q5) and, secondly, the wall of bastion itself, must be the oldest man-made football stands in the world. Admittedly, you can't stand *in* them, as they are vertical and so you would fall off unless you're Spiderman, but you can stand *on top* of them, which in my book still counts. It's shameful, a national disgrace even, that neither Sportscene nor Match of the Day has ever set up cameras there. In 1973 and 1974 they could have filmed me and my team (the name of which I can't remember) lose on both occasions in the first round of the Charities Cup. Not that I ever think about it. Happier memories, though, of my Stanks appearances as morning Sunday League goalie for Spittal Rovers. Three games undefeated (summers are short in Berwick). Two wins, a draw, one goal conceded and a penalty save. Celtic and glory beckoned, and beckon still. I know exactly what you're thinking; at 57 with left leg sciatica he has no chance. But here's a fact and a half for you. When he played for Celtic in the 1967 European Cup final, William Wallace, give or take a year or two, was 700 years old, and he had recovered from being hanged, drawn and quartered. Marvellous people, these physiotherapists. The application of simple mental arithmetic will tell you I have at least 643 years left to be spotted by a scout for the Bhoys. Plenty of time.

But wait. Standing on the curtain wall path looking over the Stanks we see that running the length of the eastern side of the pitch is a low masonry wall, on which spectators stand. And then, Bloody Berwick in hand, we look at the plan on page 144 and see a broken line running, approximately, down the middle of the pitch through the centre circle, representing the line of the medieval Edwardian walls. Some archaeologists believe when the wall was demolished its masonry was applied in the construction of the new low wall which bounds the side of the pitch, thus making this wall the oldest football stand (in the literal sense of something on which you stand) in the world, pre-dating the Elizabethan stands by the best part of three centuries.

Our next stop, where our two walks join, is above Cowport (Q5). The gate is one of four by which control over access to the town was exercised. The others were Scotsgate, which as we've seen faces Scotland; Shoregate (now Sandgate), which leads to the river mouth and which we'll pass over in a short while; and Bridgegate, which sadly is no more. It was situated at the town end of the bridge. Cowport led to coastal pasture land, Magdalene Fields. Until the early eighteenth century, all the gates were permanently guarded and closed every night at ten o'clock.

Cumberland to Brass

A view of Brass Bastion from Cumberland Bastion. The long section of wall between the two bastions is the 'curtain'. The recess is the 'flanker'. The other section of wall is the western 'flank' of Brass.

From Cowport, a short walk brings us to Windmill Bastion (Q6), similar in design but slightly larger than Cumberland, facing east to the sea. There are numerous gun placements in and around Windmill, most if not all of which date from the late nineteenth and early twentieth centuries.

Walking along the top footpath from Windmill, the earthen bank on your left has within it the remnants of a citadel which another Edward (he was Edward VI, son of and successor to Henry VIII) had constructed. It was demolished when the Walls were built. If you want to have a closer look, go down the stone steps you see in front of you and follow the path as it bends to the left. After only a few yards, adjacent to a park bench, the citadel is marked by the smallest of plaques, which might win a prize for brevity but nothing else. It reads: 'Site of Edward VI Citadel'.

Back up the steps and on to the top footpath, the next and last of the bastions comes into view. It is a demi-bastion, King's Mount (Q7). Built in 1560-61, the bastion looks over the estuary and would, therefore, have been the first line of defence against any invasion by sea. King believes it was given its current name (previously it had been known as Hundson's mount) in honour of James number six of Scotland and one of England, who passed through the town in April 1603 *en route* to his London enthronement (of which more in Chapter Thirteen). For reasons I do not know, it is the most neglected of the bastions.

King's Bastion brings us to the end of our Queen's Walk for, on leaving it, we find ourselves again following the line of the medieval walls, although that is not what was intended when Elizabeth's Walls were built. Back to the plan on page 144. Initially, it was planned that the lower part of the town, approximately south of what is now Silver Street and Bridge Street, would be left outside the Walls, which would run in a straight line from King's Mount to Meg's Mount. Have a look at the dotted line on the plan on page 144. Work commenced but, for reasons of cost, was soon abandoned, and thus the Edwardian walls along the estuary front were left in place.

The Kings' Walk – Part Two

Having passed through an iron gate beyond King's Mount, we are back following the line of the medieval walls, although what we see dates from later times. Our first stop on this section is Fisher's Fort (K6). The design you see dates from the late eighteenth century. Six cannon protected the estuary from the feared Napoleonic invasion that never happened. The one cannon still on display is Russian, a trophy from the Crimean War, captured at the siege of Sevastapol in 1855.

Coxon's Tower (K7), formerly known as the Bulwark in the Sands, is next. Its present shape dates from the eighteenth century. Cannon were placed on either side of the tower to provide additional protection for the estuary. Leaving the tower and following the path towards the Old Bridge, the cannon placements may be clearly seen.

The path passes over Sandgate and, arriving at the town end of the Old Bridge, we're more or less back to where we began. Barrels is still there, even more inviting than it was when we started out, and across the road from it is our starting point, the junction of Bridge Street and West Street. Time for a pint.

Double Indemnity

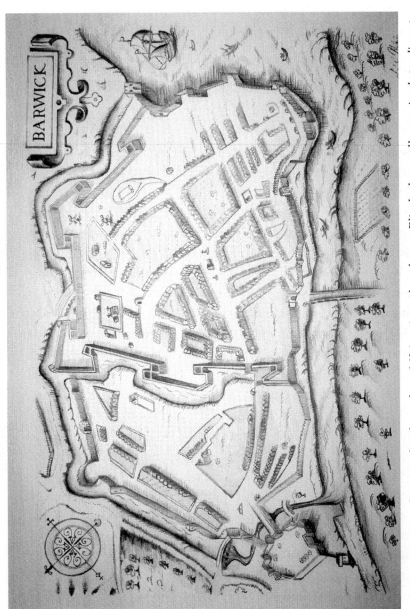

This is John Speed's town plan from about 1624, a time when the pre-Elizabethan walls remained standing at least in part. In the bottom, left-hand corner is the castle from which the Edwardian wall, incorporating both Bell Tower and Lord's Mount, can be clearly seen.

Chapter Thirteen
Peace at Last, But Where is This Town, Berwick-upon-Tweed?

Pay very careful attention to what follows. This is the denouement, where all is resolved, where after three centuries of conflict between the kingdoms of England and Scotland the union of the two crowns brings peace to Berwick, and where we find the answer to the question that down the generations has exercised the minds of our greatest historians, geographers, politicians, ethnomethodologists, phenomenon-ologists, sociologists, philosophers, theologians, and constitutional lawyers; where exactly is this town, Berwick-upon-Tweed?

But first things first. Upon completion in or about 1566, the Walls, with 54 cannon along their length, together with a town garrison of a thousand plus made Berwick the most fortified town in Europe. It was ready for a fight, a fight that never came, because while in England Tudor Elizabeth had consolidated her rule and strengthened her country militarily (the Walls being the foremost example of the same), in Scotland Stewart Mary's fortunes had taken a distinct turn for the worse, partly at fate's hands and partly as a result of her unrivalled ability to pick the wrong man.

And yet the decade had started so well for Mary, having in January 1560 become Queen Consort of France on her dauphin husband Francois succeeding to the French throne. These were worrying times for Elizabeth, to which one of her responses was to seek an alliance with Protestant Scotland against their joint enemy, the Papist King of France and his Papist wife. Elizabeth succeeded. In mid-1560, a treaty was entered into whereby if the Scottish Protestants sought to expel the not insignificant number of French forces from their country, a land army and naval support would be forthcoming from England, and if there were to be a French-backed invasion of (and note the distinction) *'the north parts of England, on the north part of the water towards Scotland'* or *'against Berwick on the north side of the water of the Tweed,'* troops from Protestant Scotland would be sent into the field and kept there if necessary for a period of 30 days, all at the Scots' own expense.

Elizabeth needn't have been so concerned. Francois died on 5th December 1560, leaving Mary immediately relegated from triple 'A' royal celebrity status to a mere 'A', or possibly even worse – horror of horrors – 'B'. Fate had dealt her a cruel blow. She then proceeded, in the several years that followed her widowhood, to turn adversity into ruin by marrying a minor aristocratic ne'er-do-well, then marrying his murderer, losing the Scottish throne to her infant son (our James number six and, subsequently, one) and becoming Elizabeth's prisoner in England, a queen without a crown.

The nearest Mary got to Berwick was as a visitor in summer of 1566, when on a progress through south-east Scotland, in the company of 800 troops and 1,000 horsemen, she paid homage at Halidon Hill to the slain of 1333, and moved from there to a spot where she could view the jewel she would never possess. The garrison knew she was there, and saluted, or depending on your view, warned her off, by a friendly discharge of cannon fire.

For Berwick, the consequence of Mary's fall was that the Walls (whisper it) became something of a white elephant. A Franco-Scottish invasion failed to materialise, and, despite the occasional scare in later centuries – a not very real threat of a Napoleonic invasion being an example – the Walls were destined never to have a shot fired in anger from them, though that is not to say they haven't witnessed the occasional coming together of opposing forces; teenage fumblings being probably the most common.

If the orders given to the town garrison are even a remotely accurate reflection of what day-to-day life was like at the time, we can say with some confidence that, for the soldiers, life was not much fun. In John Scott's *'Berwick-Upon-Tweed: The History of the Town and Guild (1888)'* there is a comprehensive list of the rules and regulations to which they were subject. Here are some of the highlights, and remember, to be found guilty of treason invited a sentence of death by hanging, drawing and quartering.

Do your duty or else	*'if there be any soldier that hath rule of the watch bell and if he make not his due haste and come to the church and strike a general larum at all such times as the said cause shall chance or require by night, he so offending to suffer death'*
Scots keep out	*'if any Scotch born person, chartered or unchartered, present themselves for to be soldiers of this garrison or take upon them to be of the stand watch, search watch, front watch, or harrage or scourage or other dutie that calls upon him or them for to come upon the town walls by night or ditches of the same, he or they so founde or taken to put to death as traytors'*
No fraternisation	*'if an English man lead any Scottish man or other aliant upon the walls of the said town by day or upon the dykes, he for his so conducting to loose all his goodes and to be banished from the town for ever and if he do any such by night he to be taken as a traitor'*

Hands off the town's married women

'noe soldier shall be suffered to keep any other man's wife or concubine but upon any vehement presumption he shall be discharged by the Governor and put out of the towne'

Gambling is permitted, provided you understand the rules

'if there be any soldier of this garrison that either dice or card for any money or play at marbles but for beer, ale, or wine either by day or by night whether in the town as well the players as the owners of the said table, dice, or cards in whose house they play, they all so offending to be imprisoned for the space of three days and whatso they have lost everie pennie thereof that to be delivered into the hands of the Captain by sufficient search as often as that cause shall require except it be within the twenty one days of Christmas or ells at any of the gates of the said town, or within water-houses or market-place or the towel bougheth of the same, he or they that otherwise do, that money and everie pennie thereof to be employed by the Captain's command went to the use of the Queen's Bridge of the said town of Berwick'

Cutting the grass, however, is not permitted

'if any soldier take upon him to mawe or cause to be mawed any grass within the bounds of the town without it be to him permitted by the Captain or counsel of the same he or they so offending to loose the said grass and for the presumption thereof to be three days in prison and if he be efstoones found in such like *fault for to loose his grasse and his roome and what wages whatsoever he be abled unto'*

Was the queen a secret Celtic supporter?

'if there be any soldier of this garrison that is abled and admitted by the captain to take the Queen's wages and if they have not a jacket of the Queen's colour, white and green, and that to wear at all such season and tymes as he shall have summons from the said captaine, he or they having no such jacket and wear that for the first default to loose three days wages and for one day to be imprisoned and for the second time to be dismissed out of wages.

After 21 years a prisoner, Mary exited our stage in February 1587, by way of execution at Fotheringhay castle in Northamptonshire. The castle, coincidentally, was the birthplace of the devil. If you have forgotten all about him and wish to be reintroduced you'll have to read Chapter Ten again. Elizabeth exited peacefully of melancholy and old age on 24th March 1603. By doing so she left the stage open for our final entrant, James number six of Scotland and, about to be, James number one of England. He had been waiting in the wings for nearly 37 years, 36 of them as king of Scotland. Now was his moment, and his starting place was, yes you've guessed it once again, Berwick.

News of Elizabeth's death travelled, relatively speaking, fast, reaching Berwick on 26th March, the day before James learnt of it. In Berwick, the great and the good, sensing they were about to play minor roles in this final act of our story, wrote to James in as obsequious terms as they could muster. This is the first part of the mayor's letter:

'Barwick, 26 Mch, 1603. Most gracious and our sole redoubted Sovereigne, fforasmuch as it hath pleased the heavenly disposer of earthly kingdoms to take to his mercy our late most gracious Sovereigne Lady Queen Elizabeth, and in exchange of a transitory crowne to bestow Vppon her an immortal diadem. And where it hath pleased the Lord to settle the hearts of the true-hearted nobilitye and Commonall State of this now your Hignes Realm of England by Mutuall Vnamite and free consent, to publish ant proclayme your most sacred Maiesty the Indubitate heire and Lawfull successsore of the Monarchall crowne of the said Realme of England.

'Wee, your Maiesty's most humble and hearty affection-ate subjects, the Mayor, Aldermen, and Commons of his Hignes Towne of Barwick-Vppon-Tweede, immediately Vppon true notice had of her Hignes decease, as well in Loyall zeal to your Maiesty as in full approbation of the said State and Counsells pendant publication, thought it our humble duties, and in like sort did with present expedi-tion publish (and with what solemnitye the leasure of time would afford) and proclayme your sacred Maisety King of England, Scotland, ffrance, and Ireland, Defender of the Faith...'

James replied the following day, in equally effusive terms, and by doing so an interesting possibility (for me at least) is raised. First his reply:

'Trusty friends wee greete you heartily well; we render you thanks for your soe dutiful affection, utterit in assist-ing and concurring sa willinglie with your Governor in putting the town of Berwick in our hands, whilk we have

appointed to be governit in the same forme and manner as
heretofore, while we advise otherwise to dispose uppon the
same ... From Hallirudhouse this 27 March, 1603.'

On 28th March, James despatched the Abbot of Holyrood to Berwick
to take possession of the town on his behalf, the Mayor and Governor
duly obliging the same day.

It is generally accepted the news of Elizabeth's death was first broken to James in the late night hours of 27th March by Sir Robert Carey,
who rode from London on 24th March and arrived at Holyrood on 27th,
falling off his horse near Norham and sustaining a severe head injury in
the process. This is the interesting question: did James already know,
courtesy of the Mayor of Berwick's letter? The letter must have been
sent by some form of express delivery, evidenced by the fact that James
penned his reply on 27th March. It is only 57 miles from Berwick to
Edinburgh, a distance that could be covered quickly by messenger on a
half-decent horse. My guess is that the messenger would have reached
Holyrood in the early to mid-morning of 27th, thereby relegating Carey
into second place in the breaking news league.

On 5th April, James set off from Edinburgh for his coronation in
London, in the company of 500 attendants, Scots and English. On 7th
April he and his retinue arrived at Berwick. And it is only right, surely,
that we should allow our dear friend, Frederick Sheldon, a witness to
so much of the bloody turmoil to which the town had been subjected
in the preceding three centuries of warfare, to describe the scene as
his friend – the gentle King Jamie as he affectionately refers to him –
entered Berwick.

'Being arrived at the boundary of the town, he was received
by Sir John Carey with every demonstration of respect and
joy, accompanied by all the officers of the town and gar-
rison and at the head of their respective companies, both

horse and foot. As his Majesty passed them, they saluted him with a discharge from their pieces; at the same time, the castle and garrison of Berwick and the ramparts commenced firing their ordnance, as the King entered the town amid acclamations of joy that, mixed with the thunder of artillery, deafened the air. He was met at Scotch Gate by William Selby, gentleman porter, who, kneeling, delivered to him the keys of the town, which his Majesty immediately returned, and knighted him forthwith. Passing on down the High Street, he arrived at the market place, through the armed bands of the garrison that lined the entire street, where he was received and welcomed with every demonstration of loyalty by Hugh Gregson, mayor of the burgh, who presented his Majesty with the gold chain of office and the charter of the town; after which the Recorder addressed the King in congratulatory speech, all of which the King received very graciously, at the same time restoring their charter, and assuring the town of his royal favour and protection...

...The bond of blood between England and Scotland was at length torn asunder; the ambition of so many kings of England was at length realised: chance by a woman's death, effected what millions of lives expended bloodily on a stricken field, had failed to accomplish. The crowns of England and Scotland were one; and James the Sixth and First was the sole monarch of the double throne... and [Berwick's] palmy days of battles and sieges became but a tale of yesterday.'

James stayed in Berwick for one full day, 8th April, during which time he was taken on a tour of the Walls and accepted an invitation to fire one of its 54 cannon, an act of some courage for a man known for his timidity and who no doubt had in the back of his mind the fate of James number three at the siege of Roxburgh.

On 9th April, by way of the rickety wooden bridge known as the Queen's Bridge (for which, as we've seen, miscreant gambling garrison soldiers contributed towards its upkeep) across the Tweed, James entered England and Northumberland. He was not impressed, with the bridge that is, not the beautiful village of Tweedmouth. *"Is there never a man in Berwick that can boo stanes to build a brig over Berwick stream,"* he is reported to have complained as the dilapidated structure swayed in the wind and tide.

For the garrison, Sheldon's 'tale of yesterday' came very quickly. Once wee Jamie was settled safely in London, orders were given to reduce the size of the garrison to a mere one hundred soldiers. Many of the officers were dismissed; others were offered posts elsewhere, Ireland being the most common destination. Those who remained suffered a reduction in pay. By 1611, all that was left of the garrison was a small number of pensioner soldiers on half pay, whose number gradually decreased to nil as nature took its course. As was the way of things then, and now some might say, material capital was valued more highly than human capital. In contrast to the casual casting off of the garrison soldiers, some of whom had served in the town throughout Elizabeth's reign, very careful attention was paid to the town's highly valuable ordnance. Much of it was removed to the Tower of London. The Walls were left naked, devoid of purpose.

There is a myth James was so traumatised by the experience of his crossing of Berwick's rotten timber bridge that he ordered a stone replacement so that, if he ever had cause to return to Scotland, he would not put his life in peril when crossing the Tweed. It is not true. In all likelihood, he forgot all about the bridge until five years into his reign, when he received a communication prepared by the town's surveyor that, in February 1608, *'a spate rose here and brought the ice so fast upon the Bridge as ten pillars and eleven bayes thereof being in the strength of the river was the thrust and caryed away'*. In his report, the surveyor recommended that a replacement stone bridge would be a more cost effective alternative than expending monies on the repair of the wooden structure, which no doubt would require yet further repair before very long. To his enormous credit, and perhaps remembering his promise of extending to the town his royal favour and protection, James agreed. On 23rd May 1608 he ordered the building of a stone bridge, funded by way of Crown subsidy.

The construction project did not get off to the most auspicious of starts. By February 1610, two partial collapses into the Tweed had been of sufficient seriousness to jeopardise the continuation of this grand exercise in public works, and had it not been for James' patience and willingness, in the face of what these days would be called misuse of public funds (i.e. corruption), in 1611 to restructure how the work was financed, the whole project would, quite literally, have been washed away by the river. From 1611, extremely close supervision and auditing by the Treasury of how monies were spent permitted consistent, if still slow, progress to be made (so slow that one cleric wit observed *"the expenses of his Majesty's monies rise apace, but the Bridge riseth slowly"*) over the next decade until, in October 1621, there was another setback:

> *'There came an extraordinary time of abundance of raine and stormes that made such floods all through the north partes as the like thereof hath not been known in any man's memory, and the River of Tweed bringing down with it a strange abundance of stacks of hay, corne and timber bore down on a great part of the old timber bridge there; which, together with the violence of the waters and abundance of stuff that came therewith falling upon the stone bridge, being yet greene and the lime not dried and knit, and the centres of some of the arches being not stricken, but standing, overthrew all the works done this year.'*

Not, happily for the town, a complete disaster, but enough to delay completion and see his Majestie's expenses riseth even further; the £12,000 already spent was supplemented by an additional capital allowance of £3,000, which was sufficient to provide for the completion of the bridge in 1624, a physical, material representation of the union of the crowns, and a foreshadow of the further union of the two countries within the United Kingdom a century later. Sadly, there is no account of the official opening ceremony (disappointingly, Sheldon refrains from imagining one). For the record, it has fifteen arches, measures 1,164 feet in length and is seventeen feet wide. If any of the aforementioned facts are wrong, blame Sheldon, not me. It stands 50 to 60 yards down river of the timber bridge it replaced – the Old Old Bridge, if you prefer. Some claim the timber foundations of the Old Old Bridge may be seen at low tide. If you spot them, let me know.

Unity in stone

Here it is, the Old Bridge, for four centuries benefiting generation after generation in countless taken for granted situations, the physical manifestation of the union of the crowns, and subsequently of the kingdoms.

And that, dear reader, is that. Finished. The end. No more. The end of a tale told by an idiot, full of facts and occasional minor embellishments, signifying not very much except, I hope you will agree, the writer's enduring affection for his place of birth. Time to take a walk up to the Cemetery Loanin to spend a short while with my mam and dad, and James and Derek. I'll pass a minute or two as well with the uncles and aunties, the Ainslies, Mitchells and Stewarts. Afterwards, a visit to Wallace Green to pay my respects to Braveheart, followed by a pint or two in the Pilot and then a good night in the Free Trade.

If you like, you can stop reading now. I won't be offended. You've made it to the end of our story and you may well have decided it's time for you to make an exit, though not of course in the same fashion as our players in Bloody Berwick. Alternatively, you can carry on reading for a few pages, and, in the short exposition which follows, discover the answer to the question posed in our chapter title; where is this town, Berwick-upon-Tweed?

Assuming you haven't exited, to answer the question we're going to step outside the three-century period that has given us our story, going back as far as the tenth century and forwards into the twentieth century. In doing so, we're going to review the constitutional position of the town by reference to how it was referred to in peace treaties after 1482 and in statutes enacted over the several centuries following the union of the crowns in 1603, to which we shall apply some expert, insightful legal analysis (that will be a first for you, then, Mr Ryan, I can hear the Northampton County Court district judges chuckle to themselves).

Our starting point is the Tweed. It became the acknowledged border between the two kingdoms of Scotland and in England in the reign of Malcolm I of Scotland, which is to say some time in the years between 943 and 954. In medieval times the status of the river as border was enshrined in the legal maxim, applicable in both England and Scotland, 'filum aquae', where the mid-point of a stream or river was assumed to be the boundary between two parcels of land. Throughout all the upheavals and changing of hands Berwick endured after Malcolm's reign until the devil took the town in 1482, no one ever argued that the border had shifted; on those occasions when the town was in English hands it was understood by all that Berwick was a Scottish town in England's possession. And it is that understanding which explains the post-1482 provision found in all peace treaties pertaining to the town up to the point of unification of the two crowns in 1603 in the person of wee Jamie. I'm sure you've memorised the said provision and can recite it perfectly in Latin, but just to remind ourselves it was this: *'Per dictum illustrissimum regem anglia vassalos sive subditos regni aut inhabitants nullam & castrum Berwice quoscumque'*. The provision invites the idea, as Ridpath, explains to us (Chapter Twelve, page 131) that from 1482, because of the distinction in the provision between the *'subjects of the illustrious king of England'* and the *'inhabitants of the town or castle of Berwick'*, the town was not considered as being within the kingdom of England. Ask yourself this question; if Berwick was in England, why was it necessary in the post-1482 treaties to insert a sub-clause expressly referring to the inhabitants of the town? It is not a question that can be answered easily. Ask another question; why was it that in the said treaties the subjects of the king of England and the folk of Berwick were mentioned separately? The answer is straightforward; they were regarded as separate, discrete peoples. The evidence of the time points to Berwick being a neutral zone. The town had a special status, persuading one chronicler – Rymer in his *Faedera* – to describe Berwick as *'a free town independent of both states'* and Sheldon to wax lyrical as only he can – *'...and Berwick, the bone of contention, the ambition of the English and Scotch to possess, about whose time-worn turrets flitted the shades of the Edwards, Bruce, Wallace, Baliol, and a long line of mighty warriors, was declared neutral.'*

After the union of the crowns there was, for obvious reasons, no need for any further peace treaties. However, the union had no bearing on the issue of whether Berwick was in Scotland or England. Its special, neutral status remained and, indeed, caused something of a headache to law makers, a problem that was not addressed until the passing of the Wales and Berwick Act 1746. It was a short Act. This is it in its entirety:

The Wales and Berwick Act 1746

It is hereby further declared and enacted by the authority aforesaid, That in all cases where the kingdom of England, or that part of Great Britain called England hath been or shall be mentioned in any act of parliament, the same has been and shall from henceforth be deemed and taken to comprehend and include the dominion of Wales and town of Berwick upon Tweed.

Ask yourself another question. Why was special, express reference made to Wales and Berwick? Why not, for example, make mention of London, Liverpool or Manchester? This is not a trick question. The answer is once again straightforward. London, Liverpool and Manchester, are, and always have been for so long as the concept of England has existed, in England, whereas Wales and Berwick have not. Thus, the reason they are mentioned is because they were not in England; they were merely *deemed* so to be; Wales was a separate dominion and Berwick was a separate town.

That is how matters remained until deep into the twentieth century when, by section 4 of the Welsh Language Act 1967, the 1746 Act was disapplied to Wales thus:

'Section 3 of the Wales and Berwick Act 1746 (which provides that references in Acts of Parliament to England and Wales include references to Wales and Berwick) shall have effect in relation to any Act passed after this Act as if the words "dominion of Wales" were omitted.'

The effect of this change was that Wales was no longer deemed to be a part of England for legislative purposes, but Berwick remained so until the passing of the Interpretation Act 1978, by Schedule 3 of which what remained of the 1746 Act was repealed, and from which it follows that the town of Berwick was no longer deemed to be a part of England for legislative purposes.

There is a widely held belief that the 1978 Act finally confirmed Berwick's constitutional position as being in England. It did no such thing. I have read the whole Act, in which there is actually no express reference to Berwick, except in so far as by section 25 and Schedule 3 thereof what remained of the Wales and Berwick Act was repealed in its entirety, the effect of which was that Berwick (like Wales before it) was no longer deemed to be in England. Nor has there been any piece of legislation passed since 1978 that has addressed the issue of Berwick town's constitutional status. Thus, constitutionally nothing has changed since the post-1482 treaties' provisions. The inescapable conclusion is that Berwick is not in England.

Are you convinced by the argument? Probably not. Does it matter? No, not really; to the English we're Scottish and to the Scottish we're English. But we know neither is correct. The colonialist Plantagenet Edwards, the ferocious Wallace, the fearsome Bruce, and the devil Richard all missed the point, for all of us born and brought up in the town know the real truth; no, Berwick is not in England, and, no, it is not in Scotland, it is in our blood; Bloody Berwick.

Chapter Fourteen
A Boy from Berwick

Gwyn, one of the many people who have helped me to get *Bloody Berwick* into print, suggested I write a short, final chapter, 'About the Author'. I hesitated at first, and as I write this I'm still hesitating. It could easily turn out to be too sentimental, too maudlin. On the other hand, it gives me an opportunity to explain, briefly, how Celtic, Neil Young and Bob Dylan find themselves in a book about medieval Berwick. And so, in a thousand words, and hoping it is not nine-hundred-and-ninety-nine too many, you have from the start of the next paragraph, as a good Berwicker would put it, all you need to know 'Aboot the Author.'

If you cast your mind back to the Introduction you'll recall I was born in Berwick, in Castle Hills Maternity Home on the north bank of the Tweed, the ninth of nine Ryans, and brought up in Dean Drive, Tweedmouth.

A childhood in Dean Drive meant playing football in the street under the benign gaze of the Woodyard Chimney, an industrial landmark in a largely non-industrial landscape, and on the sloping patch of grass that was the Oval, barely the size of a sixpence to an adult but Hampden Park or Wembley to an eight year old. In those impressionable childhood days my eldest brother, Perry, and several other young Berwick men left the town, metaphorically speaking on their bikes, to work in the Langley Alloys foundry near Slough, Berkshire. They made good money. One tea-time afternoon, I was sitting in the back kitchen of no. 43 with my mam, dad and brother, Michael, when in walked Perry with presents in hand. Christmas had come early. For Michael and me, inside each white gift box was a full Celtic kit; green and white hooped strips, in the old-fashioned rugby style, down to our knees; shorts down to our ankles; and socks up to our waists. Years later, in my Leicester unemployed bed-sit days, the strip kept me warm at night in my damp, mould walled Hartop Road room. Happy, responsibility free days. More importantly, the gift triggered a life-long love affair, admittedly mostly at a distance, with the Bhoys.

With a Berwick Catholic mother and an Irish-Scots Edinburgh Catholic father, I was pre-destined to spend my primary school years at St. Cuthbert's RC School, in Tweedmouth. I was the youngest truant in town. A product of my environment, I remain a Catholic, by my fingertips; faith and doubt consubstantial.

To my disgust and the amazement of all who knew me, in 1969 I passed the 11 plus – all I remember, if it is not a false memory, is a question about cowboys and indians – and ended up at the town's grammar school. Forced to play rugby instead of football was, in the early years, a form of torture. Things changed, however, as I moved into my mid-teens, by which time I had a grudging affection for the game. As for the school itself, with the Pilot on hand for the occasional lunchtime pint, my 'A' level years were passed happily in the company of good friends. There was some studying undertaken as well, though not too much, and I think it is right to give a special mention to Miss Trimmer, who, as my history teacher, whether she likes it or not, is partly responsible for *Bloody Berwick*.

Music. When I was 13 my brother, Derek, introduced me to the music of Neil Young via 'After the Gold Rush' and a year or so later, through a school friend, Bob Dylan's *Greatest Hits* entered my life. Ever since, the two musicians have remained by my side – together through life you could say – and the references I've made here and there to their songs and lyrics is my modest attempt to pay them homage.

Off to Leicester University at 18 years old in 1976, with fire in my belly, to study sociology and change the world. Soon, poverty, inequality and war would be in the past. If only I hadn't been so idle, if only the non-academic attractions of student life hadn't been so enticing, if only I knew what phenomenology and ethnomethodology meant, how different the world could have been today. Ah well, meeting friends who have remained friends for 40 years and will be so, all being well, for decades to come is sufficient compensation.

And then came work, marriage and children. Oh, the responsibility. I like to think I've coped reasonably well, though in respect of the latter two of the trilogy Hilary, Frances and Michael might have something to say.

And work? That has been spent, for the most part, in the legal profession. By the time I entered it, I knew I wouldn't change the world, but as a law centre solicitor I would perhaps help to better the lives of a few people. Except there wasn't a law centre in the land that would employ me, in consequence of which I found myself in what in the profession is referred to as private practice, and in fact it is not such a bad place to be, with clients and colleagues often becoming friends, and in some cases crutches.

Throughout, there has been Berwick. With family and friends in the town it has never been far away, and some years ago, on the train home for a family funeral, I came across Simon Schama's *A History of Britain Volume 1* account of the Hammer's 1296 sack of Berwick. Fascinating and annoying, the first because of Schama's clear enjoyment in telling the tale, and annoying because there I was, born and brought up in the town, yet ignorant of its history. That was the moment I resolved to educate myself. In time, the thought occurred that others, too, might like to know something about the history of the town. That, as I say, was a few years ago. Let's be honest. At a funeral, three thoughts come to the fore, not necessarily in this order; sadness, and as a Catholic, hope for the deceased; relief that it isn't yours; and the realisation that in time, possibly the next time, it will be. In my case, that vindictive, malign reminder of mortality, cancer, cast its shadow unexpectedly over my life in 2011. The physical and psychological consequences were a setback; it was a couple of years later before *Bloody Berwick* began to take shape. I've enjoyed researching it, I've enjoyed writing it, I've enjoyed including the song lyrics references that have made me smile, and most of all, I've enjoyed the opportunity to put on paper the fact that I am, and always will be, a proud Berwicker.

Scatter my ashes in Wallace Green

A note of thanks

It is extremely unlikely that I will ever again have an opportunity to thank publicly in writing all those people who, in one way or another, have enriched my life and, in recent years, supported me through some difficult times, and although this looks uncomfortably like an awards speech I'm going to do it regardless. So here goes.

To Frances and James, my mam and dad, for life and for family.

And to Hilary, for putting up with me for 25 years, and some more, and for encouraging me to get this far, to Frances and Michael for being Frances and Michael, and to my brothers and sisters for being, well, the Ryans, challenging though they are.

And to the earls and countesses of Leicester, all nine of them, who for more decades than I care to count have sought to persuade me the border lies north of Berwick. They are, in strict alphabetical order, Philip Bradley, Claire and Ken Bush, Duncan Clilverd (aka Big Dunc), Dick (aka Richard) Downing, Mark Goddin, Alistair North, and Andy (aka, for reasons too banal to explain, Digby) and Sandra Setters. They all make an appearance in the preceding pages. If you can find them, and provided you can furnish me with acceptable documentary evidence you purchased your copy of the book, I'll buy you a pint in The Pilot or The Harrow or the Free Trade or The Brewers Arms or Barrels or the Leaping Salmon, or all six if you're up for a good night out, with the caveat, just in case the book is a success, that by making this promise it is not my intention to enter into legal relations with you.

And to Laszlo for his brilliant illustrations.

And to Reverend George Ridpath, Frederick Sheldon and our other story-tellers.

And to Bob Dylan and Neil Young, for their musicianship.

And to Father Ed, for not giving up on a wanderer.

And to the Lisbon Lions, for 25th May 1967.

And to Dr B Khan and Mr Saleem El Rabaa, good men both, and to whom I'm deeply indebted for keeping this particular show on the road.

And to Ann, Stephen, Barbara, Ian, Ally, Susan, and Carol for R & F and the laughs that go with it.

And to Matthew, Jeremy, Charlie, Louise, Kerri, Kelsey, and Megan, and everyone else at T, where truly the sun does move across the sky.

And to you, dear reader, for getting this far. If, by any chance, you happen to have the funds, wherewithal and inclination to transform Bloody Berwick into a multi-award winning, exceptionally profitable, Edinburgh Festival or West End musical, or preferably both, please do not hesitate to get in touch.